1998

Restoring Life in Running Waters

For our academic ancestors and heirs,
and for our families,
who teach and inspire us to search for the facts,
to use them when we have found them, and to talk about them
so that others might do the same

Restoring Life in Running Waters

Better Biological Monitoring

James R. Karr • Ellen W. Chu

ISLAND PRESS

Washington, D.C.   Covelo, California

Cover photo: Griffin Creek, King County, Washington.
Photo by James R. Karr.

Library of Congress Cataloging-in-Publication Data

Karr, James R.
    Restoring life in running waters : better biological monitoring /
James R. Karr and Ellen W. Chu.
        p.   cm.
    Includes bibliographical references (p.   ) and index.
    ISBN 1-55963-674-2 (alk. paper : pbk.)
    1. Water quality biological assessment. 2. Stream ecology.
3. Nature—Effect of human beings on.   I. Chu, Ellen W., 1949-
II. Title.
QH96.8.B5K37 1999
333.91'6214—DC21   98-34886
                                                              CIP

Printed on recycled, acid-free paper

Manufactured in the United States of America
10 9 8 7 6 5 4 3 2 1

Contents

SECTION IV

For a Robust Multimetric Index, Avoid Common Pitfalls   116

SECTION V
Many Criticisms of Multimetric Indexes Are Myths   153

List of Figures, Tables, and Boxes

Figures

Tables

Boxes

Acknowledgments

THIS BOOK grew out of 25 years' research by James Karr and dozens of students and colleagues to develop and test multimetric indexes of biological integrity (IBIs). We, the authors, can thus take credit only for what this text says, not for all the excellent hard work on which it is based. Indeed, when we say *we* in this book, more often than not we mean those who have worked with Jim over the years or who use the IBI approach, not just we, the authors. Sometimes, of course, *we* means all of us—we the people of our nation, who depend on water resources.

We, the authors, wish first to thank Leska Fore, who, along with Billie Kerans, advanced the definition of IBI's statistical properties. We particularly want to thank the following other colleagues: J. Adams, P. Angermeier, C. Doberstein, D. Dudley, K. Fausch, O. Gorman, M. A. Hawke, E. Helmer, M. Jennings, D. Kimberling, B. Kleindl, S. Morley, A. Patterson, D. Ratcliffe, E. Rossano, I. Schlosser, L. Toth, and P. Yant.

We appreciate the comments, criticisms, and lively discussion from Wayne Davis, Phil Larsen, Bob Hughes, Paul Angermeier, Rich Sumner, Eriko Rossano, Kurt Fausch, Billie Kerans, Sherri Schultz, and several anonymous reviewers, all of whom helped make this a better book. We are grateful to Cathy Schwartz for drawing all the figures. The Island Press staff, particularly Barbara Dean and Barbara Youngblood, have been an immense pleasure to work with.

Finally, we must recognize those dedicated scientists and managers in federal and state agencies, especially Chris Yoder, Dan Dudley, Ed Rankin, Roger Thoma, and Jeff DeShon of Ohio EPA and John Lyons of the Wisconsin Department of Natural Resources, whose work to bring multimetric biological assessment into the real world offers inspiration to all concerned about the continuing loss of biological integrity in the nation's waters.

This book began as a report requested by Wayne Davis (Project Officer) under U.S. Environmental Protection Agency Cooperative Agreement CX-824131-01. Additional support came from U.S. Environmental Protection Agency Cooperative Agreement X-000878-01-6 (Marsha Lagerloef and Richard Sumner, Project Officers) and Department of Energy Cooperative Agreement DE-FC01-95-EW55084.S to the Consortium for Risk Evaluation with Stakeholder Participation (CRESP).

Life in Running Waters

> *Can we afford clean water? Can we afford rivers and lakes and streams and oceans, which continue to make life possible on this planet? Can we afford life itself? ... These questions answer themselves.*
>
> —Senator Edmund Muskie (1972)

RUNNING WATERS are the lifeblood of a continent. No wonder. Life, all life—from viruses to human society—depends on water. No water, no life; altered waters, altered life. The study of life in running waters reveals the history of an entire continent's landscape and foretells its ability to sustain life in the future. In North America, the story of life in running waters is sobering: the health and integrity of living systems in the continent's rivers have declined steadily for more than a century. *Restoring Life in Running Waters* is about reversing this trend.

Water bodies are not simply water; their value comes from more than the quality and quantity of liquid water. Humans depend on living waters for many essential goods and services, from drink and food to cleansing of our wastes to recreational and aesthetic renewal. One explicit statement in the United States' 1972 Water Pollution Control Act Amendments (now called the Clean Water Act) acknowledged the overarching importance of whole water bodies: "The objective of this Act is to restore and maintain the chemical, physical, and biological integrity of the Nation's waters" [PL 92-500, Clean Water Act (CWA), §101(a)].

Although some progress has been made under this law in controlling pollution coming from point sources, other pervasive causes of degradation continue to harm aquatic ecosystems. Altered water flows in dammed streams and rivers, pollution from diffuse nonpoint sources such as farms and feedlots, destruction of habitats above and alongside rivers by development or logging, and invasions by alien species have taken a severe toll on life in North America's waters. Despite the Clean Water Act's clear mandate and lofty language, the condition of living aquatic systems says we have failed to achieve the act's objectives.

The problem is that for more than a quarter century, water resource management has been dominated by outdated legal doctrines, weak implementation of good laws, and a focus on water chemistry. Yet the most direct and effective measure of the integrity of a water body is the status of its living systems. These systems are the product of millennia of adapting to climatic, geological, chemical, and biological factors. Their very existence integrates everything that has happened where they live, as well as what has happened upstream and upland. When something alters the landscape around a river's headwaters, life in lowland reaches feels the effects.

Restoring Life in Running Waters contends that the biology of waters must be taken seriously to restore or maintain the integrity of the nation's waters. Whether you think running water is for drinking, fishing, washing, flushing, shipping, irrigating, generating electricity, or making money in countless ways, keeping tabs on the water's biology makes sense. If we fail to protect the biology of our waters, we will not protect human uses of that water. When rivers can no longer support living things, they will no longer support human affairs.

Biological monitoring—measuring and evaluating the condition of a living system, or biota—is the first step in protecting life in waters or anywhere else. Biological monitoring tracks a biota's health in much the same way that the government or investors track the health of the economy. It aims to detect changes in living systems, specifically, changes caused by humans apart from changes that occur naturally. Tracking, evaluating, and communicating the condition of living systems, and the consequences of human activities for those systems, lie at the heart of biological monitoring.

To put it another way, biological monitoring identifies ecological risks that are as important to human health and well-being as the more obvious threats of toxic pollution or diseases like malaria and cholera. Halting the deterioration of the nation's waters cannot be done if we continue to behave as if our actions carried no ecological risks (Karr 1995a). A biota's condition, as revealed through biological monitoring, offers the most comprehensive indication of ecological risks in a particular place.

During a century of evolution, through changing human impacts on water and its associated resources, biological monitoring programs have taken a variety of approaches (Davis and Simon 1995; Karr 1998a). The approach at the heart of this book began in 1981 with the index of biological integrity, or IBI (Karr 1981). In much the way that economic indexes such as the Dow Jones industrial average and the index of leading economic indicators combine many financial measures to assess the state of the national economy, the index of biological integrity integrates measurements of a number of biological attributes, called metrics, to assess the condition of a place. Work by many investigators over more than two decades has demonstrated that such "multimetric" indexes are effective for assessing ecological condition in a variety of management settings; with many kinds, or taxa, of organisms; and in diverse geographic regions.

The key to building an effective multimetric index is finding the right attributes of a living system to measure. Attributes that do not change in response to human impact can tell us nothing about the consequences of human activities for a place and its biota. Metrics must be chosen on the basis of whether they reflect specific and consistent biological responses to human activities. Ideal metrics should be relatively easy to measure and interpret. They should either increase or decrease predictably as human influence increases. They should be sensitive to a range of biological stresses, not narrowly indicative of commodity production or of threatened or endangered status. Most important, metrics must be able to discriminate human-caused changes from the background "noise" of natural variation.

Successful multimetric efforts combine knowledge of a site's natural history with straightforward sampling designs and statistical analyses. Natural history—knowledge of living systems in the field—not solely a search for statistical relationships and significance drives the development of effective multimetric indexes. By focusing on attributes of living systems that give the clearest signals of human impact, multimetric indexes put life at the center of monitoring and management. And by focusing on life and on the conditions that support life, multimetric indexes make it easier to communicate with the citizens, policymakers, and agencies whose actions determine the condition of our nation's waters and lands. The extent to which better decisions are made—decisions that maintain or restore life and life-supporting systems as opposed to the status quo—will be a measure of these indexes' success.

Restoring Life in Running Waters discusses freshwater ecosystems in the United States and what biology tells us about their state. The book makes a case for using multimetric biological indexes to assess and communicate ecological health. Although such indexes are now widely used—in more than three-fourths of the U.S. states and on every continent except Antarctica—the approach has its vocal critics. *Restoring Life in Running Waters* also attempts to answer many of their criticisms.

Section I

Aquatic Resources Are Still Declining

Despite decades of efforts intended to protect water resources, and some success against certain forms of chemical and organic contamination, the nation's waters continue to decline, and the Clean Water Act's call for protecting integrity remains unanswered. The problem has been a failure to see rivers as living systems and a failure to take biology seriously in management programs. We need a new approach, one that integrates and informs us of the ways our rivers, landscapes, and society interact.

Water resources are losing their living components

Despite strong legal mandates and massive expenditures, signs of continuing degradation in biological systems are pervasive—in individual rivers (Karr et al. 1985b), U.S. states (Moyle and Williams 1990; Jenkins and Burkhead 1994), North America (Williams et al. 1989; Frissell 1993; Wilcove and Bean 1994), and around the globe (Hughes and Noss 1992; Moyle and Leidy 1992; Williams and Neves 1992; Allan and Flecker 1993; Zakaria-Ismail 1994; McAllister et al. 1997). Aquatic systems have been impaired, and they continue to deteriorate as a result of human society's actions (Table 1).

Devastation is obvious, even to the untrained eye. River channels have been destroyed by straightening, dredging, damming, and water withdrawal for irrigation and industrial and domestic uses. Degradation of living systems inevitably follows. Biological diversity in aquatic habitats is threatened; aquatic biotas have become homogenized through local extinction, the introduction of alien species, and declining genetic diversity (Moyle and Williams 1990; Whittier et al., 1997a). As recently as a century ago, a commercial freshwater fishery second only to the one in the Columbia River flourished in the Illinois River, Illinois. Now it is gone, and the one in the Columbia is nearly gone. Since the turn of the twentieth century, commercial fish harvests in U.S. rivers have fallen by more than 95%.

Even where commercial and sport catches of fish and shellfish are permitted, one can no longer assume that those harvests are safe to eat (U.S. EPA 1996a). In 1996, fish consumption advisories were imposed on 5% of the river kilometers in the United States (*www.epa.gov/OST/fishadvice/index.html*). The number of fish advisories is rising. The 2193 advisories reported for U.S. water bodies in 1996 represent an increase of 26% over 1995 and a 72% increase over 1993. For millennia, humans have depended on the harvest from terrestrial (including agricultural), marine, and freshwater systems for food. But the supply of freshwater foods has collapsed. How would society respond if agricultural productivity declined by more

Table 1. Examples from United States rivers of degradation in aquatic biota (from Karr 1995b).

Proportionately more aquatic organisms are classed as rare to extinct (34% of fish, 75% of unionid mussels, and 65% of crayfish) than terrestrial organisms (from 11% to 14% of birds, mammals, and reptiles; Master 1990).

Twenty percent of native fishes of the western United States are extinct or endangered (Miller et al. 1989; Williams and Miller 1990).

Thirty-two percent of fish native to the Colorado River are extinct, endangered, or threatened (Carlson and Muth 1989).

In the Pacific Northwest, 214 native, naturally spawning Pacific salmon and steelhead stocks face "a high or moderate risk of extinction, or are of special concern" (Nehlsen et al. 1991).

Since 1933, 20% of molluscs in the Tennessee River system have been lost (Williams et al. 1993); 46% of the remaining molluscs are endangered or seriously depleted throughout their range.

Since 1910, naturally spawning salmon runs in the Columbia River have declined by more than 95% (Ebel et al. 1989).

During the twentieth century, the commercial fish harvests of major U.S. rivers have declined by more than 80% (Missouri and Delaware Rivers), more than 95% (Columbia River), and 100% (Illinois River) (Karr et al. 1985b; Ebel et al. 1989; Hesse et al. 1989; Patrick 1992).

In 1910, more than 2600 commercial mussel fishers operated on the Illinois River; virtually none remain today.

Since 1850, many fish species have declined or disappeared from rivers in the United States (Maumee River, Ohio: 45% [Karr et al. 1985b]; Illinois River, Illinois: 67% [Karr et al. 1985b]; California rivers: 67% [Moyle and Williams 1990]). This decline, combined with the introduction of alien species, has homogenized the aquatic biota of many regions (an average of 28% of the fish species in major drainages of Virginia are introduced; Jenkins and Burkhead 1994).

Native minnows have declined while alien littoral predators have spread throughout northeastern U.S. lakes (Whittier et al. 1997a).

The taxa richness and relative abundances of dominant benthic macroinvertebrate groups change with land use. Most species of mayflies, stoneflies, and caddisflies—numerous in forested watersheds—disappear in agricultural and urban watersheds. They are replaced by midges (chironomids) in agricultural areas and oligochaete worms in urban watersheds (Lenat and Crawford 1994).

Riparian corridors have been decimated (Swift 1984).

Thirty-eight states reported fish consumption closures, restrictions, or advisories in 1985; 47 states did so in 1991. The 2193 advisories reported for U.S. water bodies in 1996 represent a 26% increase over 1995 and a 72% increase over 1993 (U.S. EPA 1996a). Contaminated fish pose health threats to wildlife and people (Colborn et al. 1990, 1996), including intergenerational consequences such as impaired cognitive functioning in infants born to women who consume contaminated fish (Jacobson et al. 1990; Jacobson and Jacobson 1996).

than 80% or if eating "farm-fresh" products threatened our health? Why then do we continue to ignore such changes in "wild-caught" aquatic resources?

Current programs are not protecting rivers or their biological resources because the Clean Water Act has been implemented as if crystal-clear distilled water running down concrete conduits were the ultimate goal (Karr 1995b). For example, at least $473 billion was spent to build, operate, and administer water-pollution control facilities between 1970 and 1989 (Water Quality 2000 1991). Yet the decline continues, and money is wasted on inadequate or inappropriate treatment facilities (Karr et al. 1985a; Box 1).

Box 1. Narrow use of chemical criteria can damage water resources and waste money. Use of biological criteria can do the opposite.

Most U.S. cities have spent decades installing wastewater treatment plants to protect water bodies from raw sewage. In primary treatment, wastes that float to the top or sink to the bottom of settling tanks are physically removed. The effluent passes into secondary treatment, where microorganisms digest the fine organic particles that remain. Neither primary nor secondary treatment removes chemicals from the effluent; compounds may include toxic industrial chemicals, pesticides, nitrates, and even pharmaceuticals excreted in human wastes (Raloff 1998). Tertiary treatment, the most expensive treatment level, is targeted at removing these chemicals. Wastewater treatment managers typically use chemical criteria to determine if the effluent they release into water bodies is safe after treatment. But those chemical criteria may still not protect regional waters.

Chlorine is added to secondary sewage effluent because it kills microorganisms that cause human disease. But the effects of this chlorine continue after the effluent is released into streams or other water bodies (Colborn and Clement 1992; Jacobson and Jacobson 1996). In three Illinois streams receiving water from a secondary treatment plant, an IBI based on fish declined significantly as residual chlorine concentration increased (Karr et al. 1985a; Figure 1); the biological effects of chlorine appeared in fish assemblages downstream of the effluent inflow (Figure 2). With chlorination (treatment phase I), IBIs were much lower downstream than upstream. In contrast, when chlorine was removed from secondary effluent (phase II), downstream and upstream IBIs did not differ significantly. Chlorine added to wastewater effluent continues to kill organisms long after the water is released. Furthermore, biological condition did not improve when expensive tertiary denitrification was added (phase III), even though this treatment brought the plant into compliance with chemical water quality standards for nitrates.

This example illustrates three important points. First, biological integrity may be damaged by too narrow a focus on chemical criteria. Second, such a narrow focus can waste money. Third, many current management approaches and policies are, in essence, untested hypotheses. Managers do not always make the effort to look for broader effects or to test beyond their initial criteria. Had managers looked for bio-

(continues)

logical effects or reconsidered the levels of chlorine in the effluent instead of assuming that their chlorine criteria worked, the biota of these Illinois streams might have suffered less.

The Taylor Creek watershed in nearby Ohio underwent a different experience (S. Malone, Ohio EPA, and W. C. High, Wolpert LLP, unpubl. manuscript). Plans to build a traditionally planned and engineered sewer system to meet chemical criteria—with pipes dug into stream channels and laid along riparian corridors to take advantage of gravity flow—were rejected by the state, which enforced biological as well as chemical criteria. State water managers recognized that the proposed sewer system would damage aquatic life. The engineers went back to their drawing boards and, working with biologists and others, came up with a plan that placed their sewer lines along existing rights of way such as roads. The new plan minimized stream crossings, designing them perpendicular to stream channels; it left buffer zones between the stream and construction activity and made erosion control, bioengineering, and environmental inspectors an integral part of the construction plan. As a result, 17 miles of stream were saved, and project planners discovered that they had also saved money. In fact, the contractors took the new methods to other projects as a way to save both money and time. Narrow pursuit of chemical criteria would have destroyed this stream and riparian corridor. But the presence—and enforcement—of biological criteria protected the stream and led to better engineering designs as well.

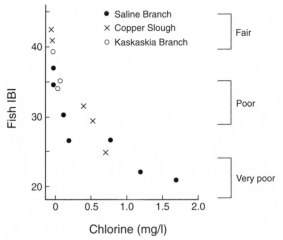

Figure 1. In three streams in east-central Illinois, the fish indexes of biological integrity (IBIs) declined significantly in response to wastewater inflow from secondary treatment with chlorination. Fish IBIs declined as residual chlorine concentration increased (from Karr et al. 1985a).

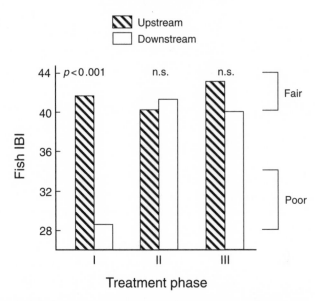

Figure 2. Fish IBIs for stations upstream and downstream of wastewater treatment effluent in Copper Slough, east-central Illinois. Phase I: standard secondary treatment; phase II: secondary treatment without chlorination; phase III: secondary treatment without chlorination but with tertiary denitrification. With chlorination (phase I), IBIs were much lower downstream than upstream of effluent inflow. Upstream and downstream sites did not differ statistically after removal of chlorine from secondary effluent (phase II). The addition of expensive tertiary denitrification (phase III) did not increase IBIs (from Karr et al. 1985a).

In many respects, society has been lulled into believing that our individual and collective interests in water resources are protected by national, state, and local laws and regulations. We have had faith in the outdated "prior appropriation doctrine" of American frontier water law, the implementation of the Clean Water Act, or "wild and scenic river" designation when, in fact, our habits as a society and the way we have implemented our laws have progressively compromised our fresh waters.

"Clean water" is not enough

Society relies on freshwater systems for drinking water, food, commerce, and recreation as well as waste removal, decomposition, and aesthetics. Yet in the Pacific Northwest alone, recent declines in salmon runs and closures of sport and commercial fisheries have led to economic losses of nearly $1 billion and 60,000 jobs per year (Pacific Rivers Council 1995). Retaining the biological elements of freshwater systems (populations, species, genes), as well as the processes sustaining them (mutation, selection, fish migration, biogeochemical cycles), is crucial to retaining the goods and services fresh waters provide (Table 2).

Waters and fish travel over vast distances in space and time. The integrity of water resources thus depends on processes spanning many spatial and temporal scales: from cellular mechanisms producing local and regional adaptations to a massive transfer of energy and materials as fish migrate between the open ocean and mountain streams. Protecting the elements and processes society values therefore demands a broad, all-encompassing view—one not yet encouraged by conventional management strategies and terminology.

In particular, the word *pollution* must take on broader connotations. In conventional usage and agency jargon, *pollution* refers to chemical contamination. A more appropriate, yet little-used, definition that more accurately represents what is at stake as water resources decline is the definition given by the 1987 reauthorization of the Clean Water Act: *pollution* is any "man-made or man-induced alteration of the physical, chemical, biological, or radiological integrity of water." Under this definition, humans degrade or "pollute" by many actions, from irrigation withdrawals to overharvesting, not merely by releasing chemical contaminants.

Table 2. Elements, processes, and potential indicators of biological condition for six levels or organization within three biological categories. Indicators from multiple levels are needed to assess the condition of a site comprehensively (modified from Angermeier and Karr 1994).

Biological category	Elements (levels)	Processes	Indicators
Taxonomic	Species	Range expansion or contraction Extinction Evolution	Range size Number of populations Population size Isolating mechanisms
Genetic	Gene	Mutation Recombination Selection	Number of alleles Degree of linkage Inbreeding or outbreeding depression
Ecological	Individual	Health	Disease Deformities Individual size and condition index Growth rates
	Population	Changes in abundance Colonization or extinction Evolution Migration	Age or size structure Dispersal behavior Presence of particular taxa (e.g., intolerants) Gene flow
	Assemblage	Competitive exclusion Predation or parasitism Energy flow Nutrient cycling	Number of species Dominance Number of trophic links Stream distance for one carbon molecule to complete passage through food chain (spiraling length)
	Landscape	Disturbance Succession Soil formation Metapopulation dynamics	Fragmentation Percentage of disturbed land Number of communities Sources and sinks Number and character of metapopulations

Biological monitoring is essential to protect biological resources

Despite their faith in and reliance on technology, humans are part of the biological world. Human life depends on biological systems for food, air, water, climate control, waste assimilation, and many other essential goods and services (Costanza et al. 1997; Daily 1997; Pimentel et al. 1997). It is therefore vital for us to assess resources in terms of their biological condition. The criteria and standards by which we judge whether an activity has an impact—the endpoints that we monitor—must be explicitly biological.

Degradation of water resources begins in upland areas of a watershed, or catchment, as human activity alters plant cover. These changes, combined with alteration of stream corridors, in turn modify the quality of water flowing in the stream channel as well as the structure and dynamics of the channel and its adjacent riparian environments. Biological evaluations focus on living systems, not on chemical criteria, as integrators of such riverine change. In contrast, exclusive reliance on chemical criteria assumes that water resource declines have been caused by chemical contamination alone. Yet in many waters, physical habitat loss and fragmentation, invasion by alien species, excessive water withdrawals, and overharvest by sport and commercial fishers harm as much if not more than chemicals.

Even measured according to chemical criteria, water resources throughout the United States are significantly degraded (U.S. EPA 1992a, 1995; see Table 1). In 1990 the states reported that 998 water bodies had fish advisories in effect, and 50 water bodies had fishing bans imposed. More than one-third of river miles assessed by chemical criteria did not fully support the "designated uses" defined under the Clean Water Act. More than half of assessed lakes, 98% of assessed Great Lakes shore miles, and 44% of assessed estuary area did not fully support designated uses (U.S. EPA 1992a).

By September 1994, the number of fish consumption advisories had grown to 1531 (U.S. EPA 1995). Seven states (Maine, Massachusetts, Michigan, Missouri, New Jersey, New York, and Florida) issued advisories against eating fish from state waters in 1994. Fish consumption advisories increased again in 1995, by 12%; the advisories covered 46 chemical pollutants (including mercury, PCBs, chlordane, dioxin, and DDT) and multiple fish species. Forty-seven states had advisories, representing 15% of the nation's total lake acres and 4% of total river miles. All the Great Lakes were under advisories. For the first time, EPA reported that 10 million Americans were at risk of exposure to microbial contaminants such as *Cryptosporidium* because their drinking water was not adequately filtered (U.S. EPA 1996c). For the same year, the Washington State Department of Ecology reported that "80 percent of the hundreds of river and stream segments and half of the lakes tested by the state don't measure up to water quality standards" (*Seattle Times* 1996). Outbreaks of *Pfiesteria piscicida,* the "cell from hell," have killed millions of fish and were also implicated in human illnesses from Maryland to North Carolina in 1997 (Hager and Reibstein 1997).

Alarming as they are, these assessments still underestimate the magnitude of real damage to our waters because they generally do not incorporate biological criteria or indicators. When compared with strictly chemical assessments, those using biological criteria typically double the proportion of stream miles that violate state or federal water quality standards or designated uses (Yoder 1991b; Yoder and Rankin 1995a). The reasons for this result are simple. Although humans degrade aquatic systems in numerous ways, chemical measures focus on only one way. Some states rely on chemical surrogates to infer whether a water body supports the "designated use" of aquatic life; others measure biological condition directly (Davis et al. 1996). Only 25% of 392,353 evaluated river miles were judged impaired according to chemical standards intended to assess aquatic life. But when biological condition was assessed directly, 50% of the 64,790 miles evaluated in the United States showed impairment. In the Piedmont region of Delaware, for example, the physical habitat and biological quality of 90% of nontidal streams is impaired (Maxted 1997). Human-made dead-end canals in residential developments along coastal bays in Delaware and Maryland support only one-seventh to one-twentieth of the species richness, abundance, and biomass of natural coastal bays (Maxted et al. 1997).

Perhaps more important, these numbers suggest that we know more about the condition of water resources than we actually do. Sadly, despite massive expenditures and numerous efforts to report water resource trends, "Congress and the current administration are short on information about the true state of the nation's water quality and the factors affecting it" (Knopman and Smith 1993). Because assessments emphasize chemical contamination rather than biological endpoints, state and federal administrators are not well equipped to communicate to the public either the status of or the trends in resource condition. Further, because few miles of rivers are actually assessed, and because those that are assessed are often sampled inappropriately (e.g., without probability-based surveys; Larsen 1995, 1997; Olsen et al., in press), percentages of impaired river miles are extremely rough at best.

In short, despite explicit mandates to collect data to evaluate the condition of the nation's water resources, and the existence of a program intended to provide an inventory under section 305(b) of the Clean Water Act, no program has yet been designed or carried out to accomplish that goal (Karr 1991; Knopman and Smith 1993). Rather, for years most state agencies operated as if more chemical monitoring were better. They continued to amass extensive data files and voluminous but indigestible reports—despite evidence that their data had little effect on water resource programs (McCarron and Frydenborg 1997). Granting permits for specific water uses, judging compliance, enforcing regulations, and managing watersheds all depend on the availability of accurate information about water resource condition. Yet agencies persisted in "studying the system to death" (McCarron and Frydenborg 1997). In many cases, by the time proof came that aquatic system health had declined, it was too late for effective prevention efforts, and restoration was too costly.

Such problems are clearly an important force driving recent state actions; 42 states now use multimetric assessments of biological condition, and 6 states are developing them. Only 3 states were using multimetric biological approaches in 1989 (Davis et al. 1996), and none had them in 1981 when the first multimetric IBI article was published. Indeed, hardly any effective biological monitoring programs were in place before 1981. Most states still have a long way to go toward collecting and using biological data to improve the management of their waters.

Because they focus on living organisms—whose very existence represents the integration of conditions around them—biological evaluations can diagnose chemical, physical, and biological impacts as well as their cumulative effects. They can serve many kinds of environmental and regulatory programs when coupled with single-chemical toxicity testing in the laboratory. Furthermore, they are cost-effective. Chemical evaluations, in contrast, often underestimate overall degradation, and overreliance on chemical criteria can misdirect cleanup efforts, wasting both money and natural resources (see Box 1). Because they focus on what is at risk—biological systems—biological monitoring and assessment are less likely to underprotect aquatic systems or to waste resources.

Biological evaluations and criteria can redirect management programs toward restoring and maintaining "the chemical, physical, and biological integrity of the nation's waters." Assessments of species richness, species composition, relative abundances of species or groups of species, and feeding relationships among resident organisms are the most direct measure of whether a water body meets the Clean Water Act's biological standards for aquatic life (Karr 1993). To protect water resources, we should track the biological condition of water bodies the way we track local and national economies, personal health, and the chemical quality of drinking water.

"Health" and "integrity" are meaningful for environmental management

Webster's dictionaries define *health* as a flourishing condition, well-being, vitality, or prosperity. A healthy person is free from physical disease or pain; a healthy person is sound in mind, body, and spirit. An organism is healthy when it performs all its vital functions normally and properly, when it is able to recover from normal stresses, when it requires minimal outside care. A country is healthy when a robust economy provides for the well-being of its citizens. An environment is healthy when the supply of goods and services required by both human and nonhuman residents is sustained. To be healthy is to be in good condition.

Despite—or perhaps because of—the simplicity and breadth of this concept, the intellectual literature is rife with arguments on whether it is appropriate to use *health* in an ecological context. Is it appropriate to speak of "ecological health" or "river health"?

The arguments mounted against health as an ecologically useful concept go something like the following. Suter (1993) insists that health is an inappropriate metaphor because it is not an observable ecological property. According to Suter, health is a property of organisms, a position that acknowledges only the first, and narrowest, of the dictionary's definitions. Scrimgeour and Wicklum (1996) believe that no objective ecosystem state can be defined that is preferable to alternative states. Calow (1992) asserts that the idea of health in organisms involves different principles from the concept "as applied to ecosystems." He distinguishes between applying the concept in a weak form to signal normality (an expected condition) and in a strong form to signal the existence of an active homeostatic process that returns disturbed systems to normality. The strong form, he suggests, requires a system-level control that does not exist in ecosystems. Neither does such a homeostatic control exist in any dictionary definition of health. Why, then, must this notion be central to health in an ecological context?

"Societal values" also enter the discussion, sometimes as an essential, sometimes as an inappropriate consideration. Policansky (1993) and Wicklum and Davies (1995) contend that health is a "value-laden concept" and therefore inappropriate in science. Yet Rapport (1989) suggests that efforts to protect ecological health must consider "the human uses and amenities derived from the system." Regier (1993) and Meyer (1997) agree with Rapport about the importance of societal values in defining and protecting health. Regier speaks of "integrity" rather than health, saying that the concept of integrity is "rooted in certain ecological concepts combined with certain sets of human values."

Other authors have searched for more objective or scientific arguments for referring to health in ecological contexts, often equating health with properties such as "self-organizing," "resilient," and "productive." Haskell et al. (1992) suggest that an ecosystem is healthy "if it is active and maintains its organization and autonomy over time and is resilient to stress." But resilience of biological systems is difficult to define and even more difficult to measure (Karr and Thomas 1996). Resilient to what? The term must be defined in the context of specific disturbances. A biota can sustain itself— it is very resilient—when faced with normal environmental variation, even when that variation is large (e.g., variation in river flow). But the same biota may not be able to withstand even the smallest disturbance outside the range of its evolutionary experience. Does this concept add any objectivity to our concept of health? In fact, highly disturbed systems tend to be resilient to stress. Does this observation mean that these systems are healthier?

Costanza (1992) goes one step further, proposing an ecosystem health index as the product of system vigor (primary production or metabolism), organization (species diversity or connectivity), and resilience (the ability to resist or recover from damage). But are these criteria scientifically defensible? Applying them, we would define lakes with limited plant nutrients as less healthy than highly productive lakes with abundant plant nutrients. Would an increase in primary production caused by the addition of excess nutrients, such as from sewage, therefore be considered still healthier? Using maximum production as a measure of ecological health is the analogue of using gross national product as a measure of economic vitality. By Costanza's second criterion, a tropical forest might be calculated as healthier (more diverse and connected) than a spruce-fir forest. By his third criterion, a community of sewage sludge worms (Tubificidae) at the outflow of a wastewater treatment plant would be healthy because it is very resilient to additional disturbance. These criteria all imply that "more is better" and can thus be turned too easily on their heads to justify human actions—from introducing species to adding fertilizers—that in fact degrade living systems.

Health as a word and concept in ecology is useful precisely because it is something people are familiar with. It is not a huge intuitive leap from "my health" to "ecological health." Cells; individual humans, animals, and plants; and complex ecological systems are all products of evolution. We understand that cells and individuals can be healthy or unhealthy; why is it unreasonable to extend the concept to ecosystems?

Of course we must "operationalize" the term—define it and find ways to measure it—but as a policy goal, protecting the health and integrity of our landscapes and rivers has a believable chance of engaging public interest and support. It is no accident that protecting biological or ecological "integrity" is the core principle of the Clean Water Act, Canada's National Park Act, and the Great Lakes Water Quality Agreement between the United States and Canada. Words like *health* and *integrity* are embedded in these laws because they are inspiring to citizens and a reminder to those who enforce the law to keep their minds on the big picture: the importance of living systems to the well-being of human society.

We contend that we can define *health* and *integrity* to make the terms useful in understanding humans' relationship with their surrounding ecological systems. Integrity applies to sites at one end of a continuum of human influence, sites that support a biota that is the product of evolutionary and biogeographic processes (Figure 3). This biota is a balanced, integrated, adaptive system having the full range of elements (genes, species, assemblages) and processes (mutation; demography; biotic interactions; nutrient and energy dynamics; and metapopulation, or fragmented population, processes) that are expected in the region's natural environment (Karr 1991; Angermeier and Karr 1994; Karr 1996). Adopting integrity as a management goal means aiming for a system that resembles this evolved state as much as possible (Angermeier 1997).

This definition of integrity takes into account three important principles: (1) a biota spans a variety of spatial and temporal scales; (2) a living system includes items one can count (the elements of biodiversity) plus the processes that generate and maintain them; and (3) living systems are embedded in dynamic evolutionary and biogeographic contexts. This breadth is important because human society depends on, and indeed values, both parts and processes—that is, both structure and function—in these systems (counter to Meyer's [1997] argument).

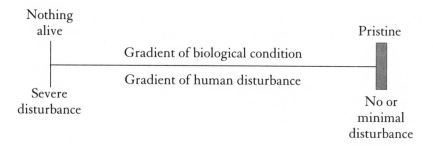

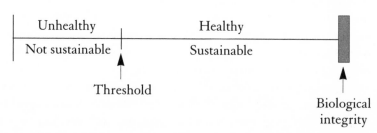

Figure 3. At one end of a continuum of human influence on biological condition, severe disturbance eliminates all life. At the other end of the gradient are "pristine," or minimally disturbed, living systems (*top*); these systems possess biological integrity. A parallel gradient (*bottom*) from integrity toward nothing alive passes through healthy, or sustainable, conditions or activities. Below a threshold defined by specific criteria (see text), the conditions or activities are no longer healthy or sustainable in terms of supporting living systems.

As human activity changes biological systems, they—and we along with them—move along a continuum, ultimately to a state where little or nothing is left alive (see Figure 3). Whether such a shift is acceptable to society is certainly a "value" decision—do we value the elements and processes that are lost?—but those decisions ought to be grounded in broad understanding of the consequences of loss, which include the loss of our own basis for existence (Westra 1998).

Two criteria would help set the thresholds for whether a loss is acceptable (Karr 1996). First, human activity should not alter the long-term ability of places to sustain the supply of goods and services those places provide. Second, human uses should not degrade off-site areas, a provision that requires a landscape-level perspective. Such criteria in decisions about environmental policy—from land use to fish harvest quotas—would avoid the depletion of living systems.

Like health and integrity generally, river health can take on multiple definitions. To irrigators, rivers are healthy if there is enough water for their fields. For a power utility, rivers are healthy if there is enough water to turn the turbines. For a drinking-water utility, rivers are healthy if there is enough pure or purifiable water throughout the year. To fishers, rivers are healthy if there are fish to harvest. For recreationists, rivers are healthy if swimming, water skiing, and boating do not sicken people. But every one of these viewpoints is only part of the picture. Each trivializes the other views of the river—not to mention nonhuman aspects of the river itself—while assigning value only to its own. To protect all river uses and values, we need broader definitions of river health.

Water bodies with integrity, especially rivers, have persisted in and shaped their region's physical and chemical environment over millennia. The very presence of their natural biota means that they are resilient to the normal variation in that environment. Still, the bounds over which the system changes as a result of most natural events are narrow in comparison with the changes caused by human actions such as row-crop agriculture, timber harvest, grazing, or urbanization. Normal, or expected, conditions constituting integrity vary geographically because each river's biota evolves in the context of local and regional geology and climate and within the biological constraints imposed by the organisms with access to that region (see Premise 6). Understanding this baseline must be the foundation for assessing change caused by humans. Only then can we make informed decisions in response to the question, Is this level of change acceptable?

When human activities within a watershed are minimal, the biota is determined by the interaction of biogeographic and evolutionary processes. As human populations increase and technology advances, landscapes are altered in a variety of ways. Those changes alter the river's biota and thus the entire biological context of the river, causing it to diverge from integrity. In some cases, the changes are minor. In others, they are substantial; they may even eliminate all or most of the plants and animals in a river. That much divergence from integrity is not healthy for humans or nonhumans.

Consideration of river health or integrity rarely entered decision making by societies bent on conquering some frontier. Water was simply there, a potable liquid to be used. It was there to be allocated, to be consumed, and to be discarded and, as likely as not, carried society's unwanted wastes with it. When the goal is to conquer, everything else is in the way. This attitude has threatened and continues to threaten the tenuous balance between water and human society, between rivers and the people who depend on rivers.

In some instances, water is at the center of, even a weapon in, age-old power struggles among humans: between the powerful and the weak in a single society—downstream populations of Hokoham in the arid American Southwest fortified themselves against upstream neighbors to retain control over the flow of water (Pringle 1998)—and between the societies of haves and of have-nots (Donahue and Johnston 1998). The consequences for human culture and values, as well as for human and ecological health, have been catastrophic.

Society—oblivious to either human-health or ecological risks of radically altering rivers—has chronically undervalued their biological components. We have behaved as if we could repair or replace any lost or broken parts of regional water resource systems, much as we replace toasters, cars, jobs, and even hearts or livers. This disregard has only worsened the lack of coherence in water law and in regulations regarding water use. The result is a body of federal, state, and local law that fails to make the connections between water quality and quantity, surface water and groundwater, headwater streams and large rivers, and the living and nonliving components of aquatic ecosystems. This disconnectedness was one thing when there were few people living on a vast North American continent; now it is quite another.

We need a new approach, one based on new conceptual models of how rivers, landscapes, and human society interact. Mental models guide much that we do. But models—whether conceptual, physical, or mathematical—can be wrong when they make inappropriate assumptions or focus on the wrong endpoint. They can mislead when they contain inappropriate levels of detail, or they can be irrelevant if they do not apply to the real world. The first rule of modeling is to recognize that "all models are wrong, but some models are useful" (Anderson and Woessner 1992). Models are most useful when they are routinely evaluated to determine if expectations are being met and if policies based on those models are accomplishing the goals of the society using those models.

A new model, with biological integrity and ecological health at its core, should inform society not only about the condition of rivers and the landscapes they run through, but also about the lives of people living in those landscapes. That model should focus on biological endpoints as the most integrative measures of river health. Because they can be defined on the basis of objective criteria (Karr 1996; Westra 1998) and used systematically to diagnose ecological condition (Rapport 1998), the concepts of biological integrity and ecological health can and should be central to that model (Rapport et al. 1998). Biological monitoring with these concepts at its core integrates the influence of all forms of degradation caused by human actions and can thus guide diagnostic, curative, restorative, and preventive management actions.

Section II

Changing Waters and Changing Views Led to Biological Monitoring

BIOLOGICAL MONITORING is evolving as societal and scientific thinking evolves. Growth in knowledge about aquatic systems—and humans' effects on them—has provided a substantial body of theory as well as empirical evidence about how to measure the systems' condition. Multimetric biological indexes synthesize and integrate that expanding knowledge. The goals of biomonitoring include improving risk assessment and risk management.

Changing waters and a changing society call for better assessment

At the end of the nineteenth century, discharge of raw sewage was a major cause of water resource degradation in the United States. Concern about the effects of excessive organic effluent on the potability of water, the spread of disease, navigation, and the status of fish populations led Congress to pass the 1899 Rivers and Harbors Act, also called the Refuse Act. The act's goal was to clean human wastes and oil pollution from navigable waterways. Protection of the nation's waters thus came under the jurisdiction of the U.S. Army Corps of Engineers.

During the world war years and afterward, legal, regulatory, and management programs concentrated on controlling organic effluent and a growing array of toxic chemicals; declining populations of sport and commercial fishes and shellfish were also targeted. Technology to clean water and to produce more fish became the watchword. Point sources of pollution were dealt with by wastewater treatment using "best available" or "best practical" technologies (Ward and Loftis 1989). Although the dust bowl of the 1930s prompted an early effort to protect water resources from nonpoint pollution due to soil erosion, soil and water conservation continued to take a back seat to augmenting agricultural production (Thompson 1995).

From the mid-1800s, hatcheries were built and operated because, like agriculture, they promised control over production and, thus, unlimited numbers of fish through technology. Technological arrogance fostered a proliferation of hatcheries (Meffe 1992), masking the degradation of river environments that was happening at the same time; yet some of that very degradation was caused by the hatcheries themselves (White et al. 1995; Bottom 1997). It was not until the 1970s—encouraged by growing public environmental awareness and passage of the 1972 Water Pollution Control Act Amendments—that management strategies began to recognize waters as a whole and to see the need to protect "the integrity of water" (Ballentine and Guarraia 1977).

The past 30 years have brought important gains in the science of water resources. Societal values, too, have been changing as human-imposed stresses have become more complex and pervasive. In addition to sewage and toxic chemicals, the nation's freshwater environments have suffered from physical destruction, increasing water withdrawals, the spread of alien species, and overharvest by sport and commercial fishers. The names and language of water laws—Refuse Act, Soil and Water Conservation Act, Water Pollution Control Act, Clean Water Act—reflect both society's changing values and attempts to cope with widening problems. Field monitoring and assessment programs have been evolving as well (Karr 1998a).

Early water quality specialists developed biotic indexes sensitive to organic effluent and sedimentation (Kolkwitz and Marsson 1908); this focus continues in modern biotic indexes (Chutter 1972; Hilsenhoff 1982; Armitage et al. 1983; Lenat 1988, 1993). The most common approach involves ranking taxa (typically genus or species) on a scale from 1 (pollution intolerant) to 10 (pollution tolerant). An average pollution tolerance level (the biotic index value) is expressed as an abundance-weighted mean for each site sampled to facilitate comparisons among sites. Some classifications use only three levels; others (Armitage et al. 1983) classify to family, calculate an average score per taxon, and reverse the scale (1 is pollution tolerant, and 10 is pollution intolerant).

An analogue for marine systems, the "infaunal index" (Wood 1980; Mearns and Wood 1982), uses four classes based on tolerance to organic effluent; the resulting biotic index ranges from 0 (all collected specimens are pollution tolerant) to 100 (all collected specimens are pollution sensitive; Ferraro et al. 1991). Two other indexes based on similar principles are a "floristic quality index," first developed in Illinois for terrestrial plants (Swink and Wilhelm 1994; Wilhelm and Masters 1995) and now used in Michigan (Herman et al. 1997) and Ohio (Andreas and Linchvar 1995; S. Fennessy, Ohio EPA, pers. commun.), and a "wetness index" (Herman et al. 1997) for wetland plants. In both cases, plant species are classified according to their tolerance to disturbance by human activity.

As toxic chemicals became more widespread, water managers recognized the limitations of early biotic indexes and began to screen for the biological effects of synthetic as well as "natural" chemicals. Biologists experimentally exposed fish or invertebrates—typically fathead minnow (*Pimephales promelas*) or *Daphnia* spp.—to contaminants, then documented the responses to create dose-response curves for individual chemical toxicants. For a given body size, they observed, very low doses of a contaminant might lead to little or no response (e.g., few or no deaths among a group of individuals). As dose increased, response increased. The goal was to establish quantitative chemical criteria to use in water quality standards. These criteria were presumed to protect human health or populations of desirable aquatic species by keeping toxic compounds below harmful concentrations—the dilution solution to pollution.

But just as biotic indexes measure primarily the effects of organic pollution, chemical criteria based on toxicology apply only to chemical contamination and a small number of contaminants. Toxicological studies, the foundation for chemical criteria, typically examine the tolerances of only a few species, usually the most tolerant taxa, leading to underestimates of the effect of a contaminant in the field. Chemical criteria based on dose-response curves for single toxicants cannot account for synergistic or other interactions of multiple chemicals in the environment. And criteria for one species do not ensure protection for others not tested. Moreover, an exclusive focus on toxicology ignores other human impacts on aquatic biota, such as altered physical habitat or flow patterns.

Much early work to detect the influence of human actions on biological systems emphasized abundance (or population size or density) of indicator taxa or guilds, often species with commodity value or thought to be keystone species. Some recent work in Scotland has successfully used standardized counts of a bird (the dipper, *Cinclus cinclus*) to indicate biological and chemical status of flowing waters influenced by acid deposition (Logie et al. 1996).

Generally, however, population size varies too much even under natural conditions to be a reliable indicator of biological condition. Such variability seems especially pronounced in comparison with physical or chemical water quality attributes. Data from long-term studies of marine invertebrates, for example (Osenberg et al. 1994), show that temporal variability for population attributes (e.g., densities of organisms) is about three times as high as for individual attributes (e.g., individual size or condition), and nearly four times as high as chemical-physical attributes (e.g., water temperature, sediment quality, water-column characteristics). Such high variability makes analyses of population size problematic for general monitoring.

Efforts to overcome this problem have led to increasingly sophisticated sampling designs. Early field assessment protocols commonly used "control-impact" (CI) or "before-after" (BA) sampling designs. In CI designs, abundance is measured at unaffected control sites and at sites affected by an impact; in BA designs, abundance is measured before, then after the event of interest. Despite the strength of these designs, the high variability of population size still makes it difficult to distinguish between changes caused by the event and variation that would occur naturally in time or space.

Population size changes in complex ways in response to changes in natural factors such as food supply, disease, predators, rainfall, temperature, and demographic lags. Increasingly complex designs (e.g., BACI; Green 1979) were developed to separate the effect of human activity from other sources of variation in time or space. But BACI confounds interactions between time and location (Smith et al. 1993); knowing the magnitude of the interaction and whether the effects are additive is critical to interpreting biological patterns—for example, understanding whether different streams respond in different ways to the same human activity. Still other statistical approaches were proposed to deal with such challenges: "before-after-control-impact paired series" (BACIPS; Stewart-Oaten et al. 1986) and "beyond BACI" (Underwood 1991, 1994). (See Schmitt and Osenberg [1996] for an excellent review of these sampling designs and their use.)

Use of these designs for biological monitoring raises a number of difficulties. First, even though assigning samples to treatment and control groups may account for local spatial variation in doses of contaminants, contaminant dispersal from a point source may be better detected by a more sensitive "gradient design" (Ellis and Schneider 1997)—that is, one that ensures sampling from sites across a range of contaminant levels. When many human activities interact and influence biological systems in complex ways across landscapes, sampling across sites subject to various degrees of influence will often be more appropriate for discerning and diagnosing the complex biological consequences of that influence (see also Premise 30).

A second, and the primary, difficulty posed by designs like BACI is the initial decision to focus narrowly on something as variable in nature as population size. In studies to determine environmental impacts, the interaction between variability and the size of the potential impact (effect size) must also be taken into account, because that interaction affects statistical power (Osenberg et al. 1994). High variation in population size, even in natural environments, interacts in complex ways with changes in abundances stimulated by human actions. Thus it can be very difficult to detect and interpret the effects of human actions even with these advanced designs. The minimum level of sampling effort may exceed the planning, sampling, and analytical capability of many monitoring situations. By shifting the focus to better-behaved indicators such as changes in taxa richness, loss of sensitive taxa, or changes in trophic organization, it is possible to use even the less complex of these designs.

When ecological research embraced species diversity as a central theme in the 1960s, diversity indexes (e.g., Shannon, Morisita, Simpson) came into vogue for evaluating biological communities (Pielou 1975; Magurran 1988).

Not long afterward, however, Hurlbert (1971) raised concerns about the statistical properties of these indexes; others later questioned their biological properties (Wolda 1981; Fausch et al. 1990; Cao et al. 1996). Diversity indexes are influenced by both number of taxa and their relative abundances; some are more sensitive to rare taxa, others to abundant taxa. Different diversity indexes may therefore produce a different rank order for the same series of sites, making it impossible to compare the sites' biological condition. Further, diversity indexes are often inconsistent because they respond erratically to changes in assemblages; thus they can lead to ambiguous interpretations (Wolda 1981; Boyle et al. 1990).

Measures of diversity were nevertheless advocated for water management (Wilhm and Dorris 1968). Florida established water quality standards based on a diversity index, although the state is now moving away from them in favor of multimetric evaluations (Barbour et al. 1996a; McCarron and Frydenborg 1997). The index of well-being (IwB), a sum of diversity indexes based on number of individuals and biomass (Gammon 1976; Gammon et al. 1981), has not been widely used, except by the Ohio Environmental Protection Agency (Ohio EPA) (Yoder and Rankin 1995a). Few scientists or managers recommend these diversity indexes today, largely because approaches are available that are both biologically more comprehensive and statistically more reliable. Unfortunately, however, diversity indexes have left a negative semantic legacy that surfaces whenever the word *index* appears (e.g., Suter 1993).

Recognizing the need for approaches better suited to considering the many attributes of biological condition simultaneously, many water resource managers have turned to two techniques with very different strengths: multivariate statistical analysis and multimetric indexes. Combinations of the two methods can be useful (e.g., Hughes et al., in press). Multivariate analysis was developed to facilitate detecting patterns, not assessing impact. Multimetric indexes, on the other hand, were designed specifically to document which components of biological systems provide strong signals about human impact and to use those signals to define biological condition and diagnose the factors likely to have caused any degradation.

Multivariate statistics "treat multivariate data as a whole, summarizing them and revealing their structure" (Gauch 1982: 1). Many researchers advocate multivariate analyses of field assessment data because these approaches are assumed to be the most objective. (Premise 33 discusses some drawbacks and misuses of multivariate analyses.) Indeed, multivariate statistics are useful when an exploratory survey is called for (Karr and James 1975; Larsen et al. 1986; Whittier et al. 1988); they can help uncover patterns when only a little is known about the underlying natural history of a place or a biota (Gerritsen 1995). But because scientists know a great deal about streams and landscapes, invertebrates and fish, and the effects of humans on those places and organisms, this book advocates actively and explicitly applying that knowledge in choosing which biological attributes to monitor and which analytical tools to use—the approach taken in developing multimetric indexes.

Multimetric indexes build on the strengths of earlier monitoring approaches, and they rely on empirical knowledge of how a wide spectrum of biological attributes respond to varying degrees of human influence. Multimetric indexes avoid flawed or ambiguous indicators, such as diversity indexes or population size, and they are wider in scope (Davis 1995; Simon and Lyons 1995).

The biological attributes ultimately incorporated into a multimetric index (called metrics) are chosen because they reflect specific and predictable responses of organisms to changes in landscape condition; they are sensitive to a range of factors (physical, chemical, and biological) that stress biological systems; and they are relatively easy to measure and interpret. The best multimetric indexes explicitly embrace several attributes of the sampled assemblage, including taxa richness, indicator taxa or guilds (e.g., tolerant and intolerant groups), health of individual organisms, and assessment of processes (e.g., as reflected by trophic structure or reproductive biology).

Multimetric indexes are generally dominated by metrics of taxa richness (number of taxa), because structural changes in aquatic systems, such as shifts among taxa, generally occur at lower levels of stress than do changes in ecosystem processes (Karr et al. 1986; Schindler 1987, 1990; Ford 1989; Howarth 1991; Karr 1991). For example, in an experimental study of North Carolina streams dosed for three years with an insecticide, changes in the numbers of mayfly, stonefly, and caddisfly taxa closely tracked changes in ecosystem processes (e.g., rates of leaf litter processing, storage of organic matter, generation and export of fine particulate organic matter, and secondary production) from pretreatment to treatment and recovery periods (Wallace et al. 1996). The taxa richness metric was relatively simple to obtain and displayed a "remarkable ability to track secondary production of invertebrates in the treatment stream" (p. 140), without the complex field and laboratory work needed to determine secondary production rates.

A multimetric index comprising well-chosen metrics integrates information from ecosystem, community, population, and individual levels (see Premise 13; Karr 1991; Barbour et al. 1995; Gerritsen 1995). Such a multimetric index clearly discriminates biological "signal"—including the effects of human activities—from the "noise" of natural variation. Finally, the result can be expressed in numbers and words to give an accurate statement about biological condition, as the following work in King County, Washington, has illustrated.

Standard samples of invertebrates from one of the best streams in rural King County contained 27 taxa of invertebrates; similar samples from an urban stream in Seattle contained only 7 taxa. The rural stream had 18 taxa of mayflies, stoneflies, and caddisflies; the urban stream had no stoneflies or caddisflies and only 1 mayfly taxon. The rural stream had 3 long-lived taxa and 4 intolerant taxa, but the urban stream had none. The rural stream had 17 taxa of "clinger" insects; the rural, none. No predatory taxa were present in the urban creek, but 12% of individuals from the rural creek were predators. When these and other metrics were combined in an index based on invertebrates, the resulting benthic index of biological integrity (B-IBI) provided a numeric description of the condition, or health, of the streams. The B-IBI for the rural stream in King County was 44 (maximum index possible, 50); that for the urban stream, 10 (minimum index possible, 10).

Biological monitoring detects biological changes caused by humans

The aim of any resource evaluation program is to distinguish relevant biological signal from noise caused by natural spatial and temporal variation (Osenberg et al. 1994). In ambient biological monitoring of water resources, signals of biological condition are measured and used to predict impacts of human activity on aquatic systems. But not all attributes of these systems, or all analytical methods, provide signals that reveal patterns relevant for managing water resources. In choosing biological indicators, one should focus on attributes that are sensitive to the underlying condition of interest (e.g., human influence) but insensitive to extraneous conditions (Patil 1991; Murtaugh 1996). Faced with a dizzying number of variables, disturbances, endpoints, and processes, water managers and researchers have periodically failed to choose those attributes that give the clearest signals of human impact. The nation's waters declined as a result.

This confusion is not difficult to explain. Like all scientists, biologists in the field are always eager to explore new places, catalogue new habitats and their inhabitants, and apply new principles in the name of "baseline research." Most scientists want to know more, rarely questioning the desirability of more research or basic research. But confusing the perspectives and goals of basic and applied ecological research has been a major reason that biological monitoring programs have seldom halted resource degradation. Compounding this problem, water managers have long sought surrogate measures of human impact or resource condition. The search for surrogates was often too narrow, and much that humans do to degrade resources was overlooked.

Basic-research ecologists try to understand natural variation over space and time within communities of organisms, along with the evolutionary and thermodynamic principles that mediate this variation (Holling's "analytical ecology" [1996]). For the most part, they work in natural systems subject to relatively little influence from human activities. They ask questions such as, Why does the number of species vary from place to place on the surface of the Earth? What regulates the size of animal and plant populations? How do global biogeochemical cycles regulate ecosystem structure and function?

Like taxonomists trying to distinguish, identify, and name species, basic-research ecologists try to distinguish unique habitat types, communities, or ecosystems and to classify them. They have long interpreted differences among environments in terms of changing species composition or abundances and energy flow or nutrient cycling; they focus on differences attributable to natural biogeographic and evolutionary processes. They identify indicator species—for example, species diagnostic of a particular type of natural community, biome, or environment (e.g., sand or gravel heathlands, alluvial grasslands, or tall- or short-grass prairie; Dufrêne and Legendre 1997). Sometimes their goal is to identify priority areas for conservation, but more often they are monitoring changes within a particular habitat. The new methods developed by Dufrêne and Legendre (1997), for example, use species-level indicators based on two criteria: specificity (association with a specific habitat type or condition) and fidelity to that habitat (McGeoch and Chown 1998). This approach is fine as far as it goes, but the emphasis on species as indicators overlooks the value of many other biological attributes in providing strong, reliable signals about biological condition.

Applied ecologists also seek to recognize natural variation, but they focus on how natural systems respond to human activities—in particular, how humans can manipulate natural systems to achieve certain ends. For the past several decades, most applied ecologists have stayed on the "engineering" side of their discipline. They have concentrated on producing higher crop yields; increasing the water supply or purifying contaminated water; or enhancing fish productivity by building hatcheries and removing woody debris from streams or, later, putting it back in. They have raised waterfowl harvests by building wetlands or engineering mitigation for wetland losses. Many applied ecologists back the intentional introduction of alien taxa, as in fish-stocking programs or "natural" pest control programs, often with substantial negative effects (Simberloff et al. 1997). Even conservation biologists have narrowly aimed to protect endangered species—as just another rare commodity—instead of seeking to protect life-support systems more broadly. Despite public awareness and legislation prompted by visibly degraded biological systems, applied ecology generally still pursues its commodity goals.

Against this scientific backdrop, public environmental policy has for many years been driven primarily by narrow physical and chemical principles. When biological targets entered the policy arena, they too were narrow (cleaner water, hardier corn, more ducks). This problem persists despite clear mandates such as the Clean Water Act's call for protecting biological integrity and despite the rhetoric of "ecosystem management" that has surfaced in the past decade. Part of the problem lies squarely with ecologists trained to see narrow commodities as their primary indicators; the solution will come from applying ecology to find better, broader indicators of biological condition.

A broader applied ecology should, for example, seek to discover the consequences of activities such as grazing, logging, and urbanization on particular places. Applied ecologists should ask, What do we measure to understand responses to human activities? What methods and measurements best isolate from noise the signal produced by human impact? How do we interpret the results? What are the likely consequences of changes we see? How do we tell citizens, policymakers, and political leaders what is happening and how to fix it? These questions form the basis of an "integrative ecology" (Holling 1996).

The first step toward effective biological monitoring and assessment, then, is to realize that the goal is to measure and evaluate the consequences of human actions on biological systems. The relevant measurement endpoint for biological monitoring is biological condition; detecting change in that endpoint, comparing the change with a minimally disturbed baseline condition, identifying the causes of the change, and communicating these findings to policymakers and citizens are the tasks of biological monitoring programs (Figure 4). Keeping this framework in mind can help keep biological monitoring programs on track.

Both basic-research ecologists and applied ecologists are interested in the top tier of Figure 4, the baseline condition minimally disturbed by human actions. Biogeochemical processes give rise to a geophysical setting and a biota defined as possessing biological integrity (Frey 1977; Karr and Dudley 1981; Angermeier and Karr 1994). Natural geophysical settings and biotas unaltered by humans in historical times constitute the main focus for basic-research ecology, but understanding and documenting these processes and components also provide the foundation for biological monitoring studies.

In essence, understanding baseline, or reference, conditions in different places is analogous to veterinarians' learning what indicates health in different kinds of animals. "Healthy" for a lizard is not the same as "healthy" for

Physical, chemical, evolutionary, and biogeographic processes interact to produce

Physical and Geographic Context	Biological Integrity
Location	Taxa richness
Geological substrate	Species composition
Climate, Elevation	Tolerance, Intolerance
Stream size, Gradient	Adaptive strategies (ecology, behavior, morphology)

The baseline without human disturbance is influenced by

Human Activities

Land use (cities, farms, logging, grazing, dams)
Effluent discharge
Water withdrawal
Discharge from reservoirs
Sport and commercial fisheries
Introduction of aliens

which alter biogeochemical processes to influence one or more of

Five Factors

Flow regime
Physical habitat structure
Water quality
Energy source
Biological interactions

thereby altering

Geophysical Condition	Biological Condition
Land cover, Erosion rates	Taxa richness
Slope stability, Evapotranspiration	Taxonomic composition
Surface permeability	Individual health
Runoff amount and timing	Ecological processes
Groundwater recharge	Evolutionary processes

Unacceptable divergence of

Biological Condition	*from*	Biological Integrity

stimulates

Environmental Policies

Regulations, Incentives
Management
Conservation, Restoration

to protect

Aquatic Life

Figure 4. Relationships among kinds of variables to be measured, understood, and evaluated through biological monitoring. Biological condition is the endpoint of primary concern.

a dog. Likewise, the expected *quantitative* values for indicators of ecological health in small midwestern North American streams are not the same as for Pacific Northwest streams or for large South American rivers, even though many of the same biological attributes may work as indicators in those disparate situations (e.g., taxa richness, relative abundance of predators). Knowing geophysical setting and undisturbed biological condition—in other words, knowing what produces and constitutes biological integrity—must underpin any biological monitoring effort.

Through time, geophysical setting and biological integrity are altered by natural events, so that over evolutionary time, biogeochemical processes may change the conditions defining regional integrity. But the rapid growth of human populations and their technologies during just the past 200 years has been a new, radically different force for change. Regional biological systems are no longer what they were 300 years ago, and the change threatens the very supply of goods and services humans depend on (Hannah et al. 1994; Costanza et al. 1997; Daily 1997; Pimentel et al. 1997).

Faced with this state of affairs, ecologists must alter the scientific backdrop. The historical dichotomy between basic ecology and applied ecology must give rise to a seamless "new ecology." Whereas basic ecology has tried to understand the natural world and applied ecology has largely concentrated on extracting human commodities from that natural world, a new ecology would protect local, regional, and global life-support systems. This more integrative ecology shares its emphasis on human activities with the commodity branches of applied ecology. But whereas commodity ecology sought to increase human influence and to use that influence to maximize harvests of wild and cultivated species, a better applied ecology would seek to understand the biological *consequences* of human activity and to minimize the harmful ones. Understanding and communicating those consequences to all members of the human community is perhaps the greatest challenge of modern ecology.

Biological monitoring measures the condition of biological systems in the broadest sense and thus lies at the base of this new ecological backdrop. The sampling and analytical tools used in monitoring must focus on detecting and understanding human-caused change. Conceptual frameworks, protocols, and procedures designed for basic research on near-pristine systems are not necessarily those that will identify change caused by human activity. Among 20 randomly selected sites sampled for benthic insects in a cold-water stream, for example, some of the variability in the samples will have natural causes (e.g., among microhabitats within a stream reach or among reaches of streams of different sizes). Sampling itself—the use of a method, the choice of a method, or the efficiency of different field teams—contributes to measured variance (see Premise 20). But the most important source of variance is differences in human activity among segments of a watershed.

In sum, biological monitoring studies must measure present biological condition and compare that condition with what would be expected in the absence of humans. Biological monitoring documents any divergences from expected baseline conditions and associates divergences with knowledge of human activities in the area; the goal is to find out why conditions have moved away from integrity. In biological monitoring, then, managers need to evaluate five kinds of information: (1) present and (2) expected biology, (3) present and (4) expected geophysical setting, and (5) the activities of humans likely to alter both the biology and the geophysical setting. Managers, policymakers, and society at large can use this information to decide if measured alterations in biological condition are acceptable and set policies accordingly. In other words, by identifying the biological and ecological consequences of human actions, biological monitoring provides an essential foundation for assessing ecological risks.

Ecological risk assessment and risk management depend on biological monitoring

Over the past decade or so, risk assessment has focused on human health effects, usually the effects of single toxic substances from single sources. As practiced since a 1983 report of the National Research Council (NRC 1983; see also NRC 1994, 1996; Risk Commission 1997), human health risk assessment asks five questions (van Belle et al. 1996), each with its own technical jargon:

- Is there a problem? (hazard identification)

- What is the nature of the problem? (dose-response assessment)

- How many people and what environmental areas are affected? (exposure assessment)

- How can we summarize and explain the problem? (risk characterization)

- What can we do about it? (risk management)

Responding to growing interest in ecological risk assessment specifically, EPA in 1992 issued its own *Framework for Ecological Risk Assessment* (see also U.S. EPA 1994a,b), which was superseded in September 1996 by the *Proposed Guidelines for Ecological Risk Assessment* (U.S. EPA 1996d). In these documents, EPA modifies the human health assessment terminology and process to evaluate "the likelihood that adverse ecological effects may occur or are occurring as a result of exposure to one or more stressors" (U.S. EPA 1996d). The agency's framework asks questions very similar to those asked in human health risk assessment:

- Is there a problem? (problem formulation)

- What is the nature of the problem? (characterization of exposure and characterization of ecological effects)

- How can we summarize and explain the problem? (risk characterization)

- What can we do about it? (risk management)

Unfortunately, most risk assessments still take a single-source–single-effect approach, ignoring the multiplicity of stressors to which individual humans, as well as ecological systems, are subjected. In another attempt to shift government thinking in this area, a Presidential/Congressional Commission on Risk issued its *Framework for Environmental Health Risk Management* (Risk Commission 1997), which simultaneously enlarges the context for "risk" to include ecological as well as public health risks and emphasizes the importance of involving the public throughout the risk assessment and management processes.

The commission's report recommends six risk management steps. It explicitly broadens the definition of risk management to include ecological risks. It urges testing of "real-world mixtures" of pollutants, such as urban smog or pesticides left on vegetables. The report recommends looking at whole watersheds and "airsheds," and it makes specific recommendations to Congress and to regulatory agencies. It also builds public involvement into all six steps, especially in defining a problem and putting it into a public health context. The report advises risk managers and citizens to: (1) define the problem and put it in context; (2) analyze the risks associated with the problem in context; (3) examine options for addressing the risks; (4) make decisions about which options to implement; (5) act to implement the decisions; and (6) evaluate the action's results. A primary challenge is to translate these goals into assessment and protection of ecological health.

All these attempts to reinvent risk management allow, even encourage, managers to broaden the questions, context, and tools they apply to the nation's environmental challenges. And although all seem to agree that risk assessment and risk management must be iterative—that conclusions must be revisited and the process repeated so that decisions may be adjusted on the basis of new information—debate still rages over which risks to assess and the "right" way to assess and manage them.

Whatever the framework for assessing ecological risks, we argue that each step must be informed by data from biological monitoring. For accurate, relevant ecological risk assessment, the measurement endpoints (what is measured) and the assessment endpoints (the ecological goods and services society seeks to protect) must be explicitly biological. Biological monitoring provides better information about actual environmental quality than chemical and physical measures alone (Keeler and McLemore 1996), because biological attributes are one step closer to the factors that constitute environmental quality for living things. Microeconomic models based on chemical levels as surrogates of environmental quality may be useful for approximating the costs of pollution control, for example, but they are limited in their ability to explain the ecological, explicitly biological, damage caused by that pollution (Keeler and McLemore 1996). Economic models incorporating biological measures, on the other hand, can contribute more accurately to a whole-system approach to resource management.

To see the benefits of biological monitoring, consider the waste implicit in decisions to invest increasing amounts of money in wastewater treatment in North America while paying little attention to whether water resource condition was improving or to the influence of other limiting factors. The nonlinear nature of ecological systems makes conventional wastewater treatment very inefficient (Statzner et al. 1997). Eventually, environmental improvement per dollar spent declines because other factors begin to limit overall environmental quality. But judicious use of biological monitoring can track living components of the environment directly, thereby improving efficiency. Tracking environmental quality through biological monitoring can guide investment strategies toward those that would yield the greatest benefit per dollar spent. In short, the use of biological endpoints, rather than pollution control dollars or numbers of permits issued, will improve decision making, achieve greater environmental improvements for each increment of expenditure, and improve our ability to reduce ecological risks.

Ecological risk assessment will miss its mark if it simply folds ecological terminology into a new pollution control or human health–focused process (Karr and Chu 1997). To protect biological resources, we must measure, monitor, and interpret biological signals. For if we do not understand how biological systems respond—and the consequences of those responses for human well-being—we cannot understand what is at risk or make wise choices.

Section III

Multimetric Indexes Convey Biological Information

Five ACTIVITIES are central to making multimetric biological indexes effective (Karr and Chu 1997):

1. Classifying environments to define homogeneous sets within or across ecoregions (e.g., streams, lakes, or wetlands; large or small streams; warm-water or cold-water lakes; high- or low-gradient streams; depressional or flow-through wetlands).

2. Selecting measurable attributes that provide reliable and relevant signals about the biological effects of human activities.

3. Developing sampling protocols and designs that ensure that those biological attributes are measured accurately and precisely.

4. Devising analytical procedures to extract and understand relevant patterns in those data.

5. Communicating the results to citizens and policymakers so that all concerned communities can contribute to environmental policy.

Understanding biological responses requires measuring across degrees of human influence

Our ability to protect biological resources depends on our ability to identify and predict the effects of human actions on biological systems, especially our ability to distinguish between natural and human-induced variation in biological condition. Thus, even though measures taken at places with little or no human influence (e.g., only from "reference" sites) may tell us something about natural variability from place to place and through time at undisturbed sites, they cannot tell us anything about which biological attributes merit watching for signs of human-caused degradation. To find these signs, sampling and analysis should focus on multiple sites within similar environments, across the range from minimal to severe human disturbance.

One could choose sampling sites that represent different intensities of only one human activity, such as logging, grazing, or chemical pollution. It would then be possible to evaluate biological responses to a changing "dose" of a single human influence. Though rare, such a study opportunity could help identify the biological response signature characteristic of that activity (Karr et al. 1986; Yoder and Rankin 1995b). Knowledge of such biological response signatures would give researchers a diagnostic tool for watersheds influenced by unknown or multiple human activities. In reality, however, it is virtually impossible to find regions influenced by only a single human activity.

In most circumstances, diverse human activities interact (e.g., during urbanization) to affect conditions in watersheds, water bodies, or stream reaches. In such cases, sites can be grouped and placed on a gradient according to activities and their effects: industrial effluent is more toxic than domestic effluent, for example, and both pose more serious threats than low dams, weirs, or levees (Figure 5). Removal of natural riparian corridors damages streams, but conversion to a partially herbaceous riparian area is less damaging than conversion to riprap. Streams grouped this way show striking and systematic differences in biological condition across the gradient of human disturbance (Figure 6).

1. Classify sites according to the amount of effluent present.

2. Within each of these broad classes, rank sites according to the types of effluent.

3. Within each of these classes, rank sites according to proximity of dams, weirs, and levees.

4. Within each of these classes, rank sites according to riparian vegetation.

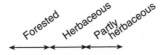

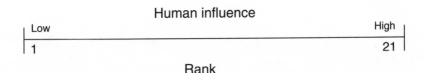

Figure 5. A priori classification system for ranking Japanese streams according to intensity of human influence (Rossano 1995). Sites were assigned to one of 21 possible categories based on amount and type of effluent, proximity of dams and other structural alterations, and type of riparian vegetation. Even without quantitative measures from each site, this approach allowed sites to be ranked across a range of human influence.

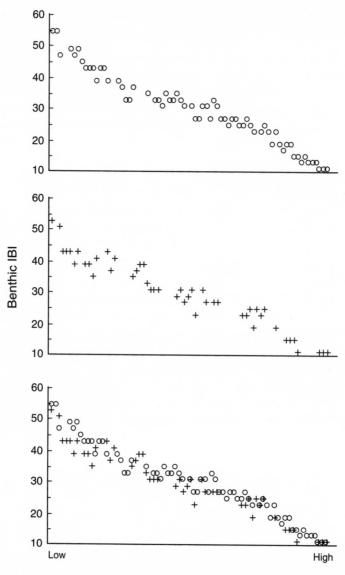

Human influence

Figure 6. Benthic indexes of biological integrity (B-IBIs) for 115 Japanese streams (from Rossano 1995). The top panel shows B-IBIs calculated from half of the 115-stream data set (circles), which was used to initially select and test metrics for use in the B-IBI. The middle panel shows B-IBI values calculated from the second half of the data set (pluses); the metrics and scoring criteria used for these data were the metrics and criteria developed from the first half. In the bottom panel, all 115 B-IBIs are plotted together; the indexes from both sets correspond closely, ranking the streams comparably according to intensity of land use from low to high. The range of human influence against which the B-IBIs are plotted comes from the classification scheme shown in Figure 5.

Sometimes a single variable can capture and integrate multiple sources of influence. Relatively simple descriptors—human population in the watershed, percentage of impervious area, percentage of land area devoted to agriculture or urban uses, or percentage of developed area—are adequate for regional watershed analyses (Meeuwig and Peters 1996). The percentage of impervious area, for example, summarizes the multiple effects of paving, building, and other consequences of urbanization, as in a recent study of Puget Sound lowland streams (Figure 7; see also Maxted 1997). This measure provides a simple surrogate of human influence that works well at percentages of impervious area from near 0% to 60%. Unfortunately, it is less useful in understanding the often large variation in biological condition at some percentages of imperviousness (e.g., 3% to 8%; see Figure 7). Finding the differences in human activity that can explain these biological differences requires information from the watersheds that is more detailed.

Alternatively, sites may be grouped into qualitative disturbance categories. In a study of recreational influence on stream biology in the northern Rocky Mountains (Figure 8), Patterson (1996) classed sites into four categories associated with different levels of human activity: (1) little or no human influence in the watershed; (2) light recreational use (hiking, backpacking); (3) heavy recreational use (major trailheads, camping areas); and (4) urbanization, grazing, agriculture, or wastewater discharge. Patterson demonstrated that light recreational activity did not substantially reduce

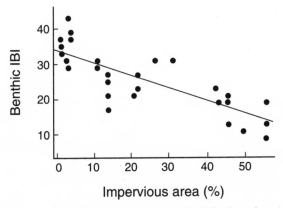

Figure 7. Benthic index of biological integrity (B-IBI) plotted against the percentage of impervious area for urban, suburban, and rural stream sites in the Puget Sound lowlands, Washington (from Kleindl 1995). Though B-IBI clearly decreases with increasing impervious area, this plot offers no insight into B-IBI differences among sites with similar percentages of impervious area, especially at low percentages (3% to 17%).

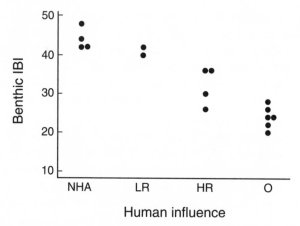

Figure 8. Benthic indexes of biological integrity (B-IBIs) for stream sites in or near Grand Teton National Park, Wyoming (from Patterson 1996). Before B-IBIs were determined, these sites had been placed into four categories of human influence: little or no human activity (NHA), light recreational use (LR), heavy recreational use (HR), and other (O). B-IBIs revealed no significant difference between sites with little or no human activity and those having low recreational use. But B-IBIs were significantly lower for sites used heavily for recreation and lower still for sites subjected to other uses—specifically, urbanization, grazing, agriculture, and wastewater discharge.

B-IBIs in comparison with undisturbed watersheds. Heavy recreational use, in contrast, did significantly alter the benthic invertebrates, although not as much as more-intensive uses including urbanization and agriculture.

A similar approach was taken in a study of biological response to chemical pollution on three continents: South America, Africa, and southeastern Asia (Thorne and Williams 1997). The authors classified sites according to a pollution gradient based on the integration of six measures of chemical pollution. Biological condition, as indicated by metrics such as total taxa richness (families) and mayfly, stonefly, and caddisfly richness, clearly went down as pollution went up. The biological responses in the three tropical regions were similar; the patterns parallel those seen in temperate regions even though the faunas are all very different.

Data collected over a number of years at the same site(s) can also reveal biological responses as human activities change during that period. Regardless of how one represents a range of human influence among study sites, sampling from sites with different intensities and types of human activity is essential to detect and understand biological responses to human influence.

The goal is to compare like environments with like environments—to isolate and understand patterns caused by human activities at sites within those like environments.

Too many existing studies confound patterns of human influence with natural variation over time at undisturbed sites or across different environment types. In other situations, researchers combine measures of human activity, the physical and chemical manifestations of those activities, and their biological consequences in a heterogeneous analysis with ambiguous results. Those analyses may even include measures of physical environment such as stream gradient. When this range of factors (different human influences on different environment types) is lumped in a single analysis, it becomes almost impossible to understand the causes or consequences of human versus natural events.

Consider the following analogy. Three experiments are designed: one to understand variation in natural biological systems as a function of stream size; another to distinguish the effects of pesticide runoff on streams of first, fourth, and sixth order; and a third to define the effects of pesticides on plants and insects. Analyzing samples from the first series of stream sites would tell you about biological responses to changing stream size. Samples from the second series would illustrate changing human influence as a function of stream size. Samples from the third would distinguish responses of different taxa. It would be silly to mix the data from the three studies in a single statistical analysis, without regard to which study the individual samples came from. Yet by using analytical procedures that mix the effects of natural and human-induced variation (in a single correlation matrix, for example), researchers are essentially doing just that: they are ignoring the context of the different components of their data, making it difficult to distinguish the biological signs relevant to resource management or protection. They then confound the sources of the variance they see, even if their initial sampling setup would have permitted discrimination among those sources. Univariate and multivariate analyses all too often suffer from this flaw.

Sampling only from "reference" sites creates a similar problem because it does not provide a way to document which biological attributes vary with human influence (see Premise 31). Careful thought about which variables best summarize human influence and the relationships among those variables should be the foundation of monitoring protocols. Creating opportunities to discover biological patterns in relation to human activity must be foremost.

Only a few biological attributes provide reliable signals about biological condition

The success of biological monitoring programs and their use to define and enforce biological criteria is tied to identifying biological attributes that provide reliable signals about resource condition (Table 3). Choosing from the profusion of biological attributes (Figure 9) that could be measured is a winnowing process, in which each attribute is essentially a hypothesis to be tested for its merit as a metric. One accepts or rejects the hypothesis by asking, Does this attribute vary systematically through a range of human influence? When metrics are selected and organized systematically, an effective multimetric index can emerge.

Knowledge of natural history and familiarity with ecological principles and theory guide the definition of attributes and the prediction of their behavior under varying human influences. But successful biological monitoring depends most on demonstrating that an attribute has a reliable empirical relationship—a consistent quantitative change—across a range, or gradient, of human influence. Unfortunately, this crucial step is often omitted in many local, regional, and national efforts to develop multimetric indexes (e.g., RBP I, II, III; Plafkin et al. 1989).

The study of populations has dominated much ecological research for decades (see Section II), so researchers still assume that population size (expressed as abundance or density) provides a reliable signal about water resource condition. But because species abundances vary so much as a result of natural environmental variation, even in pristine areas, population size is rarely a reliable indicator of human influence (see Premise 14 and Premise 25). Large numbers of samples (>25) were required, for example, to detect small (<20%) differences in number of fish per 100 square meters of stream surface area in small South Carolina streams (Paller 1995b). Other attributes—such as taxa richness (number of unique taxa in a sample, including

Table 3. Key terms used in defining biological condition.

Term	Definition
Endpoint	A measured characteristic that indicates the condition of a biological, chemical, or physical system
Attribute	Measurable part or process of a biological system
Metric	Attribute empirically shown to change in value along a gradient of human influence
Multimetric index	A number that integrates several biological metrics to indicate a site's condition
Biological monitoring	Sampling the biota of a place (e.g., a stream, a woodlot, or a wetland)
Biological assessment	Using samples of living organisms to evaluate the condition or health of places
Biological criteria	Under the Clean Water Act, numerical values or verbal (narrative) standards that define a desired biological condition for a water body; legally enforceable

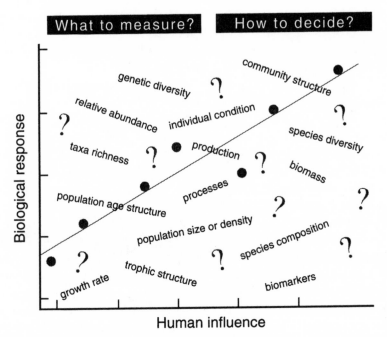

Figure 9. Almost any biological attribute can be measured, but only certain attributes provide reliable signals of biological condition and therefore merit integration into a multimetric index.

rare ones) and percentages of individuals belonging to tolerant taxa—have, in contrast, been found to vary consistently and systematically with human influence. Such attributes, when graphed, give rise to analogues of the toxicological dose-response curve—which we call ecological dose-response curves—where the y-axis represents the measured attribute and the x-axis, measures of human influence (Figure 10).

Ecological dose-response curves differ in one critical respect from toxicological dose-response curves. Toxicological dose-response curves usually measure biological response in relation to dose of a single compound. Ecological dose-response curves measure a biological response to the cumulative ecological exposure, or "dose," of all events and human activities within a watershed, expressed in terms such as percentage of area logged, riparian condition, or percentage of impervious area. The number of native fish species in a midwestern stream sampled today, for example, reflects the cumulative effects of natural events and human influence up to the present. The very existence of those species is the product of what has occurred before.

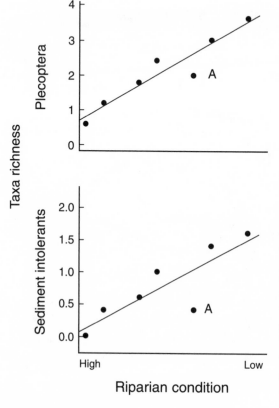

Figure 10. Average taxa richnesses of Plecoptera and sediment-intolerant taxa plotted against riparian condition for seven stream sites in the John Day Basin, Oregon, in 1988. Site A had fewer taxa than expected because although cattle were excluded, intense grazing upstream had affected the site's biota.

Graphs reveal biological responses to human influence

"Often the most effective way to describe, explore, and summarize a set of numbers (even a very large set) is to look at pictures of those numbers. . . . [O]f all methods for analyzing and communicating statistical information, well-designed data graphics are usually the simplest and at the same time the most powerful" (Tufte 1983: 9; see also Tufte 1990, 1997). Tufte's message is nowhere more important than in the display, interpretation, and communication of biological monitoring data.

Graphs reveal the biological responses important for evaluating metrics more clearly than do strictly statistical tools. They exploit "the value of graphs in forcing the unexpected" (Mosteller and Tukey 1977) on whoever looks at them, including researchers, who must then confront and explain the pattern in those graphs. For samples where the relationship between human influence and biological response is strong, statistics and graphs agree (Figure 11). In other cases, meaningful biological patterns can be lost by excessive dependence on the outcome of menu-driven statistical tests. Statistical correlation can miss an important relationship if the x-variable (e.g., percentage of area logged) is measured with low precision or if additional factors beyond those plotted on the x-axis influence metric values but are not included in the statistical analysis.

In Figure 12, for example, we plot two different aspects of biological condition against one measure of human influence, such as the percentage of upstream watershed that has been logged. Sites are assigned a plus or minus on the basis of that measure and other aspects of human influence that are visible and documented but not plotted on the same graph. In forested watersheds, these other aspects might include whether roads are near or far from the stream channel, time since logging, or traits unique to particular watersheds. In some cases, such interacting factors may degrade biological condition (roads near the stream channel would worsen logging's effects), or they may allow good conditions to persist (roads on distant ridges

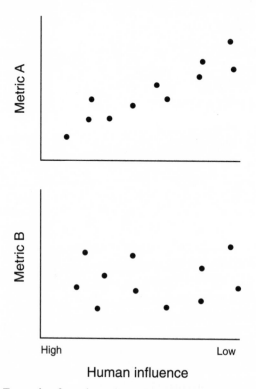

Figure 11. Example of two hypothetical metrics plotted against a gradient of human influence. Here statistical correlation and graphical analysis agree: metric A is a good indicator, and metric B is not. (Compare Figure 12.)

have less effect on streams). The distribution of pluses and boxes in Figure 12 illustrates the fallacy of assuming that a biological metric says nothing about condition because it does not correlate strongly with a single surrogate of that condition, as researchers perennially assume when a biological measure does not correlate with some measure of chemical pollution. Rather, we should conclude that the surrogate is not capturing significant components of human influence and look more closely for the biological explanations behind the data.

Not all aspects of human influence can be easily captured in a single graph or statistical test. When a number of variables influence condition, a single plot against one dimension of human influence will not tell the whole story (Figure 13); neither will a single statistical test. Graphs force us to search for insights that rote application of statistical tests cannot discover.

Weak statistical correlation can also miss important biological patterns

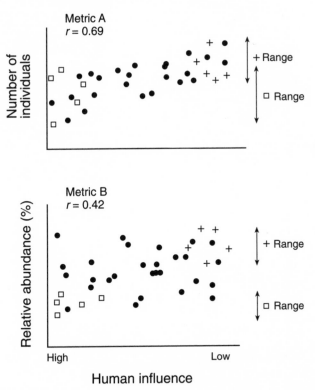

Figure 12. Hypothetical relationships between human influence and candidate biological metrics (from Fore et al. 1996). Metric A is more strongly correlated with resource condition (or r^2 is higher if using regression) than Metric B, initially suggesting that it is a better metric. But comparing the metrics' ability to distinguish between minimally disturbed sites (denoted by plus signs) and severely degraded sites (open boxes; ranges noted by arrows) shows that Metric B is actually a more effective measure of biological condition despite its smaller statistical correlation. (Compare Figure 11.)

when the distribution of the data (e.g., Figure 14) does not lend itself to tests based on standard correlation techniques that detect only linear relationships. Yet nonlinear patterns are common in field data (Figure 15). Consider the plots in Figure 16, for example. The points fall into a wedge-shaped distribution, whose scatter shows little or no statistical significance but can be interpreted biologically. The upper bound of each plot is the hypotenuse of a right triangle (the maximum species richness line) that defines the number of species expected in minimally disturbed streams as a function of stream size (Fausch et al. 1984). The plots illustrate what Thomson et al.

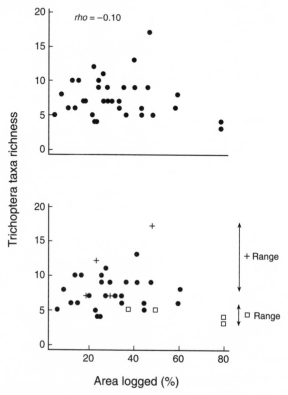

Figure 13. Taxa richness of Trichoptera plotted against the percentage of water-shed area that was logged for 32 stream sites in southwestern Oregon. Metric correlation (Spearman's *rho*) was not significant because, alone, the percentage of area logged was an inaccurate measure of human influence; other factors, such as type of logging, presence of roads, and other human influences, were not included. When these other human influences were considered, to identify minimally disturbed sites (denoted by plus signs) and severely degraded sites (open boxes), the response of Trichoptera taxa richness visibly distinguished between different degrees of human disturbance.

(1996) term a "factor ceiling distribution" (see also Blackburn et al. 1992 and Scharf et al. 1998 on ecological inferences from the edges of scatter diagrams). In this case, the ceiling—maximum species richness—is defined by the evolution of the regional biota. Generally at sites where the number of fish species falls below the ceiling, some human activity in the adjacent or upstream watershed has reduced the number of species present; alternatively, sampling might have been inadequate, "dragging" species richness below the line.

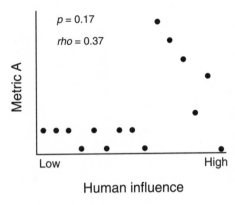

Figure 14. Hypothetical relationship between human influence and a Metric A. Statistical correlation (Spearman's *rho*) is not significant, yet the graphic pattern strongly suggests a biological response. At low levels of human influence, Metric A is not a reliable indicator of biological condition, but where human disturbance is high, the metric does respond.

Graphs highlight idiosyncrasies in data distributions that, when examined closely, may provide insight into the causes of a particular biological pattern. At one extreme, outlying points on a graph may offer key insights about the complex influence of human activities in watersheds. The researcher can then explore what unique situations at those sites cause them to appear as outliers.

Even the spread of data can offer insights, as illustrated by the large range in B-IBIs at sites with 20% to 30% impervious area shown in Figure 17. Sites with high mayfly taxa richness (B and C) lie in reaches of two streams with relatively intact riparian corridors and wetlands. The site with

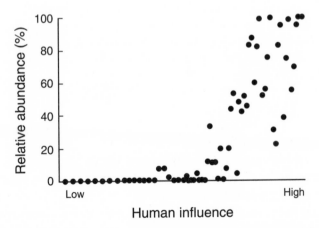

Figure 15. Relative abundance (percentage of total) of individuals belonging to tolerant taxa in samples of benthic invertebrates from 65 Japanese streams ranked according to intensity of human influence (see Figures 5 and 6). (Data provided by E. M. Rossano.)

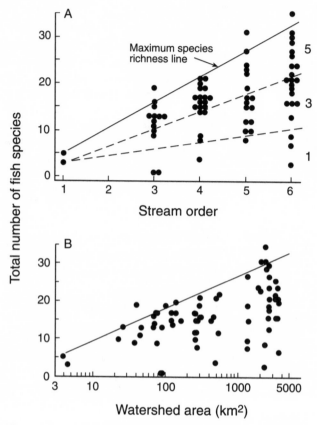

Figure 16. Number of fish species in relation to stream size (*top*) and watershed area (*bottom*); each point represents a site. The maximum species richness line through the highest points on each graph defines the number of species expected in minimally disturbed streams or watersheds. Points below that line represent sites where human activity has reduced the number of species present (from Fausch et al. 1984).

low mayfly taxa richness (A) is located in a stream that receives fine material from an old coal mine. Sites A, B, and C had unique characteristics that were best understood by examining their specific contexts, not by applying a regression or correlation analysis. Finding these patterns then led to subsequent studies in the same and in other places to determine if those patterns were more general.

Graphs also illustrate variation in behavior among taxa in response to a specific disturbance (Figure 18). For example, numbers of taxa for three

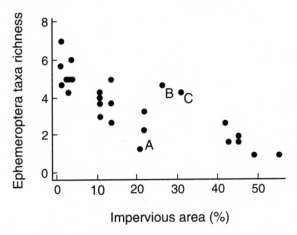

Figure 17. Average taxa richness of Ephemeroptera plotted against percentage of impervious area surrounding Puget Sound lowland streams (from Kleindl 1995). Site A, Coal Creek, had fewer Ephemeroptera than expected. This site has an active mine in its headwaters, and Ephemeroptera are known to be sensitive to mine waste. Sites B and C had relatively intact riparian areas (wetlands).

orders of insects (stoneflies, mayflies, and caddisflies) declined downstream of the outflow from a streamside sludge pond in the Tennessee Valley, but the magnitude of change varied among the taxa (see also Premise 14). The same graph also reveals the direction and magnitude of change along a longitudinal transect down the stream.

Graphs may sometimes allow researchers to avoid naive application of elaborate multivariate techniques (Beals 1973). Principal components analysis, the most often used ordination technique (James and McCullough 1990), defines statistically orthogonal factors, which may or may not be independent biologically; interpreting the results can therefore be complicated (Goodall 1954). Graphs can be a superior approach to methods that focus on maximum variance extracted because they reveal ecological rather than mathematical associations, a more appropriate criterion for organizing and understanding complex information (Beals 1973).

Complex ecological situations require unusual analytical means. Graphs can often be ecologists' most useful tools, permitting the exploration of ecological data "before, after, and beyond the application of 'standard analyses'" (Augspurger 1996). Rather than choose an inappropriately linear statistical model before plotting their data, ecologists should exploit the power of graphs for "reasoning about quantitative information" (Tufte 1983) and

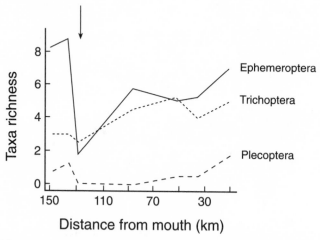

Figure 18. Taxa richness of mayflies, stoneflies, and caddisflies for sites along the North Fork Holston River in the Tennessee Valley in 1976 (from Kerans and Karr 1994). Arrow indicates the position of the streamside sludge pond. Taxa richnesses for all three orders decline at the sludge pond and slowly recover for sites downstream.

then choose and apply appropriate statistics. It is myopic to be a slave of standard statistical rules and procedures—just as it would be myopic to avoid statistics altogether.

Similar biological attributes are reliable indicators in diverse circumstances

A striking conclusion from 15 years' research in selecting metrics is that the same major biological attributes serve as reliable indicators in diverse circumstances. This result has its advantages and disadvantages. On the advantage side, every small project (e.g., at the county or community level) need not test and define its own locally applicable metrics. Scientists and resource managers can implement local biological monitoring and assessment programs on the basis of results from other studies. When local studies cite earlier work, readers can know that the methods have been tested elsewhere; the accumulating body of tests refines, or refutes, the generality of patterns that others have defined.

On the disadvantage side, some applications of multimetric indexes uncritically borrow theoretical or empirical metrics from other studies. This borrowing becomes problematic when the theory is wrong or does not apply in the study circumstance, or when metrics are applied to systems or regions other than those for which they were tested. For example, human impacts may increase taxa richness in cold-water streams (Hughes and Gammon 1987; Lyons et al. 1996), as cool- and warm-water species enter areas where water temperatures have been raised by activities that alter riparian vegetation. In contrast, in eastern warm-water streams, human influence commonly decreases species richness except for aliens (Karr et al. 1986). Thus, you cannot make identical assumptions about metrics of fish taxa richness in the two contexts.

Similarly, a benthic invertebrate metric for soft-bodied organisms (e.g., oligochaetes, tipulid flies, and other grublike forms) often indicates degraded conditions in North America, but in Japan, the better metric is legless organisms, a grouping that includes the soft-bodied organisms but also shelled snails and mussels. In North America, mussels and snails are more often indicators of high-quality environments, but in Japan, most of these taxa are alien or otherwise indicative of degraded conditions.

The bottom line is that metrics should be based on sound ecology and adapted only with great care beyond the regions and habitats for which they were developed. Exploring biological patterns to discover the best biological signals (that is, metrics) should mix graphs, conventional statistics, and thoughtful consideration of regional natural history.

Tracking complex systems requires a measure that integrates multiple factors

Policymakers, citizens, and scientists faced with making decisions about complex systems—economies, personal health, societal well-being, an ecological system—need multiple levels of information. Consider some of the indexes used to track the health of the national economy: the index of leading economic indicators, the producer price index, the consumer price index, the cost-of-living index, and the Dow Jones industrial average. All these indexes integrate multiple economic factors.

The index of leading economic indicators (Mitchell and Burns 1938) tracks the U.S. economy in terms of 12 measures: length of work week; unemployment claims; new manufacturing orders; vendor performance; net business formation; equipment orders; building permits; change in inventories, sensitive materials, and borrowing; stock prices; and money supply. These measures are combined to form the overall index, which takes as its reference point a standardized year (e.g., 1950); the value of the current year's index is expressed in terms of its value in the reference year. Composite economic indexes like these have survived six decades of discussion and criticism and remain widely used by economists, policymakers, and the media to interpret economic trends (Auerbach 1982).

Similarly, physicians and veterinarians rely on multiple measures and multiple tests to assess the health of individual patients. On a single visit to the doctor, you might be "sampled" for urine chemistry, blood-cell counts, blood chemistry, body temperature, throat culture, weight, or chest X-rays. Clearly, these measurements are not independent of one another, for they come from a single individual whose health is affected by many interacting factors. Further, you would not expect your doctor to rely on only one specialized blood test to diagnose your overall health; rather, you assume that multiple measures will give a more accurate diagnosis. Patterns emerging from these multiple measurements enable the doctor to recognize the signature of a particular ailment and to suggest more targeted measurements if she suspects a certain disease. Only then could she prescribe treatment.

Societal well-being obviously comprises many factors, not just the economic. To foster well-being, policy decisions need to consider as many factors likely to be affected by the outcome as possible. Multiattribute models have been developed to aid this kind of decision making by quantifying the effects of alternative decisions on multiple societal attributes (Gregory 1987).

Multimetric biological indexes calculated from ambient biological monitoring data provide a similar integrative approach for measuring condition and "diagnosing" causes in complex ecological systems. The same logical sequence applies in compiling multimetric economic, health, societal, or biological indexes. First, identify reliable and meaningful response variables through testing; then measure and evaluate the system against expectations; finally, interpret the measured values in terms of an overall assessment of system condition. The resulting index (for economic or biological resources) or diagnosis (for patients) allows people without specialized expertise to understand overall condition and to make informed decisions that will then affect the health of those economies, resources, or patients.

Most multimetric biological indexes for aquatic systems comprise 8 to 12 metrics,[1] each selected because it reflects an aspect of the system's biological condition. These metrics are not independent because they are calculated from a single collection of organisms, just as multiple personal health tests are done on a single individual. But even if metrics are statistically correlated, they are not necessarily biologically redundant. Rather, just as a fever plus a high white-blood-cell count reinforces a diagnosis of bacterial infection, multiple metrics all contribute to a diagnosis of ecological degradation, or ecological "disease." Moreover, when more than one metric points to similar reasons for degradation, there is less uncertainty (Smith 1994). Even when some redundancy exists among metrics, multiple lines of evidence are valuable.

The two most common IBIs for streams have been developed, tested, and applied using fish (Karr 1981; Miller et al. 1988; Lyons 1992a; Fore et al. 1994; Lyons et al. 1995, 1996; Simon 1998) and benthic invertebrates (Kerans and Karr 1994; Kleindl 1995; Rossano 1995, 1996; Fore et al. 1996; Patterson 1996). Both incorporate known attributes from multiple levels of biological organization and different temporal and spatial scales. Typically, patterns

---

[1] For species-poor environments such as cold-water streams, the total number of metrics is likely to be smaller (e.g., Lyons et al. 1996).

emerge that are the signatures of biological responses to particular human activities (Karr et al. 1986; Yoder 1991b; Yoder and Rankin 1995b).

Following the success and widespread use of these two indexes, similar indexes are now being developed by a number of state agencies to use with invertebrates and vascular plants in wetlands (Karr 1998c); with algae and diatoms in streams (Bahls 1993; Kentucky DEP 1993; Florida DEP 1996; Barbour et al., in press); with diverse taxa in lakes (Harig and Bain 1998; Whittier 1998); and with plants, invertebrates, and vertebrates in terrestrial environments (CRESP 1996; Chu 1997; Bradford et al. 1998; Blair, in press; see also Premise 22). Extending IBI to new taxa, environment types, and geographic areas is like learning to practice medicine in humans, pets, livestock, and others: the expectation of what constitutes "health" depends on the animal, but the same fundamental diagnostic strategy applies in all cases.

Multimetric biological indexes incorporate levels from individuals to landscapes

The success of multimetric approaches such as IBI in assessing biological condition depends on choosing and integrating metrics that reflect diverse responses of biological systems to human actions. Ideally, a multimetric index would cover all such responses, but the costs of developing such an index would be much too high. A set of chosen metrics is necessarily a compromise between "too narrow" and "too broad"; it is also a compromise of choices among conveniently measured biological surrogates of important biological phenomena. Metrics will evolve and expand over the next decade as researchers apply this approach in diverse regions and habitats and for different organisms. Still, a fundamental tenet of IBI is to deliberately choose metrics covering the range of biological signals available from disturbed systems.

IBI is not a community analysis in either of the common uses of the word *community*. IBI does not examine all taxa but is generally based on one or two assemblages (which Fauth et al. [1996] defines as phylogenetically related groups of organisms), such as fish or benthic invertebrates. Neither does a multimetric IBI focus on the community level in the standard textbook hierarchy of biology (individual, population, assemblage, community, ecosystem, and landscape). Rather, the choice of measures in a multimetric index reflects an attempt to represent as many of those levels as possible, preferably directly but at least indirectly. The resulting indexes are likely to produce the strongest multimetric view of biological condition (Table 4). The best multimetric indexes are more than a community-level assessment because they combine measures of condition in individuals, populations, communities, ecosystems, and landscapes.

Table 4. Types of metrics, suggested number of metrics of each type, and corresponding levels in the biological hierarchy. Well-constructed multimetric indexes contain the suggested number of metrics from each type and therefore reflect multiple dimensions of biological systems.

Metric type	Number	Individual	Population	Community	Ecosystem	Landscape
Taxa richness	3–5	✓	✓	✓	✓	
Tolerance, intolerance	2–3		✓	✓		
Trophic structure	2–4			✓	✓	✓
Individual health	1–2	✓				
Other ecological attributes	2–3	✓	✓	✓	✓	✓

Individual level. Individual health manifests itself in many ways both internally and externally, through physiological or morphological signs and metabolic or genetic biomarkers reflecting organismal stress. We have not yet seen reliable metabolic or genetic biomarkers that can be applied broadly in field studies, although in certain situations (see Summers et al. 1997 for a promising example), biomarkers may work as secondary tools for diagnosing biological condition. To date, however, IBI metrics of individual health consist of easily detected external abnormalities; their frequency in an assemblage indicates stress on individuals.

In fish, for example, visible signs of stress include skeletal deformities; skin lesions; tumors; fin erosion; and certain diseases that are associated with impaired environments, especially large amounts of toxic substances. Early studies of fish in the seven-county area around Chicago indicated high incidence of external abnormalities (Karr 1981), a pattern also apparent in Ohio (Yoder and Rankin 1995a). Among benthic invertebrates, head-capsule deformities in chironomids (midges) are strong indicators of toxics (Hamilton and Saether 1971; Cushman 1984; Warwick et al. 1987; Warwick and Tisdale 1988). Anomalies in fish are often used as IBI metrics, but chironomid head-capsule deformities are rarely incorporated into the benthic IBI because so much laboratory work is required to stain individual insects, mount them on slides, and count them.

In other studies, tadpoles collected in a coal ash deposition basin had fewer labial teeth than tadpoles from reference areas (Rowe et al. 1996). They also had deformed labial papillae, which would limit the foods they could eat and thus their growth. Fish in Gulf of Mexico estuaries showed higher numbers and frequencies of several pathologies at heavily disturbed sites than at minimally disturbed sites (Summers et al. 1997). Finally, in a metal-contaminated Rocky Mountain river in Colorado, periphytic diatoms of the genus *Fragilaria* had deformed cells (McFarland et al. 1997). The percentage of deformed cells ranged from 0.2% ± 0.2 to 12% ± 2.0 from low to high levels of contamination by heavy metals (cadmium, copper, iron, and zinc).

Population level. Several metrics in both the fish and benthic IBIs indicate, if not the details of population demography, the relative condition of component groups. Usually, a population must be viable at a site before one can consistently detect a species' presence. For example, the lack of intolerant taxa among fish or invertebrates or of clingers (taxa that cling to rocks) among the invertebrates is a strong signal that populations of these organisms are doing poorly. The absence of darters, sunfish, and suckers among the fishes and of mayflies (Ephemeroptera), stoneflies (Plecoptera), and caddisflies (Trichoptera) among the invertebrates suggests that viable populations of many species within these taxa cannot maintain themselves. The presence or absence of certain age classes, such as large old fish, among coldwater salmonids may also be a useful metric.

Assemblage level. Changes in the chemical, physical, and biological environment resulting from human activities alter assemblages. These changes may appear as changes in species composition or species richness (conventional measures of community structure). They may also appear as altered trophic structure, such as decreases in top carnivores or increases in omnivores, or as shifts from specialists to generalists in food or reproductive habits (reflecting shifts in food-web organization or changing availability of microhabitats for spawning). Multimetric indexes incorporate this information by including metrics such as the percentage of predators, omnivores, or other feeding groups and also species richness and the relative abundance of alien fishes (in streams) or of vascular plants (in wetlands and terrestrial environments).

Considerable theoretical discussion has centered on "functional feeding groups" of North American benthic invertebrates (Cummins 1974; Cummins et al. 1989; Cummins et al. 1995). In particular, according to the river continuum hypothesis (Vannote et al. 1980), the relative abundance of these groups is predicted to change along the length of a river or stream. For example, in comparison with headwaters, which are presumed to receive mostly allochthonous organic matter (from outside the stream), downstream reaches might have more filter-feeders or net-spinning caddisflies taking advantage of high in-stream production. But the river continuum hypothesis does not seem to apply consistently across North American streams (Vannote et al. 1980; Winterbourn et al. 1981; Minshall et al. 1983). Metrics based on functional feeding groups among benthic invertebrates (with the possible exception of relative predator abundance) likewise respond differently in different streams (Karr 1998b).

This inconsistent response differs from what might be a more general pattern of trophic metric behavior in fishes; perhaps the trophic structure of fish assemblages in North America is more consistent than for benthic invertebrates. Alternatively, perhaps more is known about the natural history of fishes, permitting better delineation of feeding groups. Or our knowledge of invertebrates may be less precise, or invertebrates may be more opportunistic. The generality of trophic group response to disturbance deserves more careful analysis, but, meanwhile, be careful. Despite a widely accepted theory, metrics pertaining to functional feeding groups among benthic invertebrates may or may not be good indicators; their dose-response relationships to human influence must be carefully tested and established for multiple data sets and circumstances before they should be used in a multimetric index.

Landscape level. Regardless of level in the biological hierarchy (individuals, species, ecosystem), the persistence of living things depends on heterogeneities in space and time. Spatial heterogeneities are visible in littoral zonation, in vegetation bands associated with water depth in marshes, or in association with soil moisture and slope gradients on drier land. Stream fish spend their lifetime in many microhabitats; they are exposed to different flows and other temporal shifts as days and seasons change. Eggs laid in main-channel gravels become fry hiding in side channels and along the banks. Fry grow into juveniles large enough to avoid the predators that would otherwise eat them. Juveniles may then move into the deep pools those predators inhabit and where food supplies also differ.

Finding food, avoiding predators, seeking spawning habitat—any activity in an organism's life cycle—are subject to and dependent on such heterogeneities in space and time. For some species, the scale of movements may extend only a few centimeters; for others, the scale can be hundreds or thousands of miles. The loss of spatial or temporal components of these heterogeneities can change a species' distribution or abundance, or cause it to disappear altogether. The presence or absence of anadromous or other migratory fishes (e.g., salmon, bull trout) is thus a landscape-level indicator. Dams, alien predators, and altered water flows and temperatures interfere with their movements through a landscape, decimating these species.

Incorporating several multimetric indexes (fish IBI, benthic IBI, algal IBI) into a biological monitoring program is a good way to capture the condition of assemblages that respond to human disturbances at different scales. Different taxa in the same or different assemblage reflect the presence of a broad range of heterogeneities. If top predator taxa needing large home ranges or long-lived taxa requiring years to mature are present, for example, you can infer that the spatial and temporal components they require are also present. Excessive in-stream production or numerous herbivorous fishes or invertebrates would characterize heavily grazed landscapes, where riparian corridors may be damaged and excessive nutrients from livestock wastes are entering the stream.

Development of IBI to date has involved a conscious effort to span the variety of biological contexts. But much remains to be done. Better measures of individual health are needed, as are measures better defining demographics. Strengthening the connections between measures of food web and trophic structure and more-direct measures of nutrient cycling and energy flow would also improve multimetric assessment. Finally, landscape metrics that emphasize overall biological condition (number of native community types or cumulative taxa richness across a watershed) are also needed. Ideally, metrics of landscape condition should be more than a sum of site-specific assessments.

Throughout development and use of multimetric indexes, great care must be taken to measure biological condition, not stressor intensity. Biological surrogates of biological condition are essential; chemical and physical surrogates of biological condition are not adequate by themselves.

Developed and applied properly, the multimetric IBI incorporates and depends on known components of biology—components specific to localities and taxa—across the organizational hierarchy and from disparate spatial and temporal scales. The result is a synthesis of biological signals that reveal the effects of human activities at different levels, in different places, on different scales, and in response to a range of human activities.

Metrics are selected to yield relevant biological information at reasonable cost

The index of biological integrity first developed for fish (Karr 1981; Karr et al. 1986) incorporated 12 metrics from three biological categories: species richness and composition, trophic composition, and individual condition. Later work with both fish and invertebrates led to somewhat different groupings: specifically, species richness, taxonomic composition, individual condition, and biological processes (Karr 1993; Barbour et al. 1996b) and community structure, taxonomic composition, individual condition, and biological processes (Fore et al. 1996). Within each broad category, some metrics are proven for many regions and faunas. Others work in some regions or studies but not in others. Still other potential metrics based on theoretical ecology or toxicology may work but have not been adequately tested, because they are either too difficult to measure or too theoretical to define (Table 5).[2] The categories in Table 5 guide metric selection for new regions, faunas, or habitats, but no metric should become part of a multi-metric index before it is thoroughly and systematically tested and its response has been validated across a gradient of human influence.

The choice of how to actually express each metric is as important as selecting the metric itself. You could simply count the number of individuals in a target group and express it as population size, abundance, or density (Figure 19, top); you could determine the proportion, or relative abundance, of the total number of individuals belonging to a target group

---

[2] Unfortunately, untested or too theoretical attributes have been central to EPA's rapid bioassessment protocols (RBP I, II, III), used since 1989. Many measures incorporated into RBP III were never adequately tested, and tests (Barbour et al. 1992; Kerans et al. 1992; Kerans and Karr 1994; Barbour et al. 1996a; Fore et al. 1996) now indicate that they do not meet rigorous standards for accepting metrics.

Table 5. Sample biological attributes, in four broad categories, that might have potential as metrics. Actual monitoring protocols have proven some of these attributes effective; other attributes may work but need more testing; still others are difficult to measure or too theoretical. Ideally, an IBI should include metrics in each of these categories, but untested or inadequately tested attributes should not be incorporated into the final index.

Category	Demonstrated effective	Need more testing	Difficult to measure or too theoretical
Taxa richness	Total taxa richness Richness of major taxa, e.g., mayflies or sunfish	Dominance (relative abundance of most-numerous taxa)	Relative abundance distribution, after Preston (1962)
Tolerance, intolerance	Taxa richness of intolerant organisms Relative abundance of green sunfish Relative abundance of tolerant taxa	Number of rare or endangered taxa	Chironomid species (difficult to identify)
Trophic structure	Trophic organization, e.g., relative abundance of predators or omnivores		Productivity
Individual health	Relative abundance of individual fish with deformities, lesions, or tumors Relative abundance of individual chironomids with head-capsule deformities Growth rates by size or age class	Contaminant levels in tissue (biomarkers)	Metabolic rate
Other ecological attributes		Age structure of target species population	

(number of individuals in the target group divided by the total number of individuals in the sample; Figure 19, middle); or you could count the number of taxa in the entire sample or in particular subgroups (taxa richness; Figure 19, bottom). You could also determine the proportion of the biota from specific taxa (e.g., number of mayfly taxa/total number of taxa). Approaches vary in their ability to reveal consistent dose-response

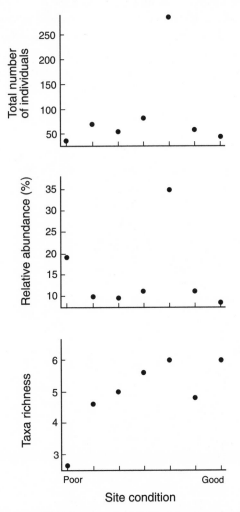

Figure 19. Presence of Trichoptera (caddisflies) in a standard sample, expressed as total number of trichopteran individuals (*top*), relative abundance of trichopteran individuals (*middle*), and richness of trichopteran taxa (*bottom*). These three biological attributes are plotted against riparian condition as an indicator of site condition at seven stream sites in the John Day River basin, north-central Oregon.

relationships, as Figure 19 shows; knowledge of natural history and of which sampling protocols are most efficient should guide your choice.

Population size—besides being difficult and often costly to determine with sufficient precision (Paller et al. 1995b), especially for rare species—is not a good measure because it is naturally too variable, irrespective of human impacts (Karr 1991). Work in Puget Sound lowland streams, for example, found no systematic relationship in two successive years between benthic invertebrate abundance and the percentage of impervious area in the upstream watershed, one measure of human influence (Figure 20).

Similarly, ratios of two groups in an assemblage do not respond systematically to human influence, largely because ratios are composed of two factors that can respond, and thus vary, independently of each other, making it

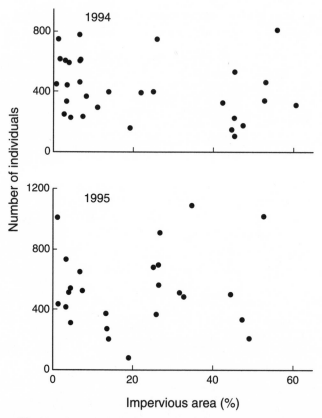

Figure 20. Number of invertebrates plotted against impervious area for lowland Puget Sound streams in two successive years.

impossible to draw firm conclusions about the relationship of the ratio to human influence (see Premise 25). Further, two large numbers and two small numbers may yield the same ratio, although the biological meaning of small and large numbers may be very different (Kerans and Karr 1994). If both components of the ratio are important, it is more appropriate to consider them separately. (This reasoning also applies in the case of diversity indexes, which combine richness and relative abundances. The attributes should be kept distinct with separate metrics.)

Metrics related to feeding ecology or trophic structure are best expressed as relative abundance—for example, the number of individual predators, omnivores, or scrapers divided by the total number of sampled individuals.[3] The relative abundance of organisms at various levels in a stream's trophic organization reflects the condition of the food web, including energy flow and nutrient dynamics, but relative abundances are much easier to measure than true production or energy flow. If we know what to expect from minimally disturbed sites in a region, we can then find the deviations caused by human activities from that expectation. The relative abundance of fish-eating fish in minimally disturbed streams, for example, is likely to be 20% or more; omnivores, 20% or less. In degraded streams, the relative abundance of omnivores is likely to be much higher (>40%).

Major taxonomic groups are best evaluated in terms of taxa richness, because as human activities damage a stream and its watershed, native taxa tend to disappear.[4] A decline in taxa richness is generally one of the most reliable indicators of degradation for many aquatic groups (Ford 1989; Barbour et al. 1995). These include periphyton (Bahls 1993; Pan et al. 1996); phytoplankton (Schelske 1984); zooplankton (Stemberger and Lazorchak 1994); river fish (Karr 1981; Miller et al. 1988; Ohio EPA 1988; Rivera and Marrero 1994; Rodriguez-Olarte and Taphorn 1994; Lyons et al. 1995, 1996; Koizumi and Matsumiya 1997); lake fish (Minns et al. 1994); estuary fish (Thompson and Fitzhugh 1986; Deegan et al. 1993; Weaver and Deegan

---

[3] Although this metric looks like a ratio, it is actually a proportion—the value of a variable divided by a constant for the sample. Proportions are more reliable as indicators because they are based on a binomial distribution (Fore et al. 1996). In contrast, the ratios of two taxa or two functional feeding groups comprise two variables from the sample; combining them in a ratio has serious statistical consequences, producing a Cauchy distribution (Hannaford and Resh 1995).

[4] Taxa richness can be standardized per unit of area (e.g., taxa per 0.1 square meter) or per count of individuals (e.g., taxa per 500 individuals). The proper choice is hotly debated, a topic we cover in more detail in Premise 29.

1996; Deegan et al. 1997; Hartwell et al. 1997); freshwater invertebrates (Ohio EPA 1988; Reynoldson and Metcalfe-Smith 1992; Kerans and Karr 1994; DeShon 1995; Fore et al. 1996; Thorne and Williams 1997); and marine invertebrates (Summers and Engle 1993; Engle et al. 1994; Weisberg et al. 1997).

An exception to this pattern arises when alien taxa are involved. The presence of alien taxa is a clear indication of human influence. Furthermore, in diverse regions, from 10% to 15% of alien taxa are considered harmful because they have "a significant impact on ecosystem health" (Mills et al. 1998). For example, of more than 4500 alien taxa in the United States, nearly 700 are considered harmful.

Taxa richness may be calculated for an entire sample or for subgroups, such as fish families or insect orders, that use the stream environment in a particular way. Sunfish, for example, feed in the water column or at the surface of pools, whereas suckers feed in benthic pool environments, and darters or sculpins feed in benthic riffle environments. Each requires the unique structural complexity and cover associated with those particular feeding environments; the interactions of cover, structural complexity, and changing food abundances resulting from human actions may cause declines in all these groups. Because their natural histories differ, these three taxa provide information about the condition of three different habitat types within a stream. Loss of sucker taxa points to a problem, such as sedimentation, within the benthic pool environment. Loss of sunfish suggests loss of physical cover and their invertebrate foods from the pelagic and surface zones of pools; indeed, insects decline at the surface when riparian vegetation is lost. Similar information may be gained from the taxa richness of lithophilous ("rock-loving") spawners or nursery species.

Among benthic invertebrates, the taxa richnesses of Ephemeroptera (mayflies), Plecoptera (stoneflies), and Trichoptera (caddisflies) reflect different types of degradation. Ephemeroptera taxa are lost when toxic chemicals like those from mine wastes foul a stream (see Figure 18; Hughes 1985; Kiffney and Clements 1994). Plecoptera taxa disappear as riparian vegetation is lost and sediment clogs the interstitial spaces among cobbles. Plecoptera tend to decline at less intense levels of human influence than Trichoptera or Ephemeroptera. Therefore, combining these three taxa into a single "EPT"[5] metric (as in RBP III and others; Plafkin et al. 1989; Lenat

---

[5] EPT is the sum of the mayflies (Ephemeroptera), stoneflies (Plecoptera), and caddisflies (Trichoptera) found in a benthic invertebrate sample.

and Penrose 1996) may obscure real differences that could help diagnose both the types and sources of degradation at a site.

The signals provided by intolerant and tolerant taxa mean that the best expression of metrics based on these taxa is not the same for intolerants and tolerants. The mere presence of very sensitive, or intolerant, taxa (as apparent from taxa richness) is a strong indicator of good biological condition; the relative abundance of intolerant taxa, in contrast, is difficult to estimate accurately without extensive and costly sampling efforts. Presence alone of tolerant taxa, on the other hand, says little about biological condition since tolerant groups inhabit a wide range of places and conditions. As conditions deteriorate, however, their relative abundance rises (see Figure 22). In general, we recommend that only about 10% (no fewer than 5% or more than 15%) of taxa in a region should be classed as intolerant or tolerant. The point of these metrics is to highlight the strong signal coming from presence of the most intolerant or most tolerant taxa, the two ends of a continuum. We avoid the average tolerance value calculated in biotic indexes because the strong signals of tolerants and intolerants are swamped by the remaining 70% to 90% of taxa with intermediate tolerances.

(For a more statistical rationale for choosing taxa richness and relative abundance, see Premise 20, Figure 34.)

Multimetric indexes are built from proven metrics and a scoring system

Across taxonomic groups, many of the same biological attributes indicate human-induced disturbance (see Premise 14; Table 6). Numerous studies have helped define the most broadly applicable metrics (Karr 1981; Miller et al. 1988; Kerans and Karr 1994; Fore et al. 1996; Scott and Hall 1997; Voshell et al. 1997; see Barbour et al. 1996b for summary table of metrics). After testing in a series of independent studies, 10 attributes of stream invertebrates and 10 to 12 attributes of stream fishes consistently emerge as reliable indicators of biological condition at sites influenced by different human activities in different geographic areas (Tables 7 and 8; see also Table 5).[6]

Consistently reliable metrics include the total number of taxa present in a sample (total taxa richness), the number of particular taxa or ecological groups (e.g., taxa richness of darters or mayflies), the number of intolerant taxa, and the percentage of all sampled individuals (relative abundance) belonging to stress-tolerant taxa (e.g., tubificid worms). Among fishes, a high percentage of individual fish with disease, fin erosion, lesions, or tumors indicates toxic chemicals in a stream. Increased frequency of hybrids seemed a useful metric in early IBI studies (Karr 1981; Karr et al. 1986), although relatively few studies since then have used it successfully. Increased hybridization could indicate a loss of habitat variety and consequent mixing of gametes from different species spawning in a homogenized environment (Hubbs 1961; Greenfield et al. 1973).

---

[6] The number of metrics in the fish IBI is somewhat smaller in relatively simple systems such as cold-water streams (Lyons et al. 1996). Wetlands may be most appropriately assessed with multiple taxa (e.g., plants, insects, fish, birds) with fewer metrics for each IBI based on a given taxon or assemblage.

Table 6. Regardless of taxon used or habitat sampled, similar metrics respond predictably (✓) to human influence. As human influence increases, taxa richness declines, the relative abundance of generally tolerant organisms increases, and generally sensitive taxa disappear. (Sources: See pages 71–72, Premise 14.)

Taxon	Habitat	Taxa richness	Relative abundance of tolerants	Number of sensitive or intolerant taxa
Fish	River	✓	✓	✓
Fish	Lake	✓	✓ (generalists)	✓
Fish	Estuary	✓		✓ (nursery specialists)
Benthic invertebrates	River	✓	✓	✓
Periphyton	River	✓	✓	✓

The values of metrics such as these provide the best and most complete assessment of a site's condition, but to compare sites and communicate their relative condition to the widest possible audience, metric values at a site are summarized in the form of an aggregate index—the index of biological integrity. Because human actions affect biological resources in multiple ways and at multiple scales, 10 to 12 metrics from four broad categories (see Tables 4 and 5) are selected and then scored using standardized scoring criteria; these metrics are the building blocks of the multimetric index (Karr 1981, 1991; Karr et al. 1986).

Because we now know a great deal about which metrics respond consistently to different levels of human effect, agency biologists with limited budgets do not have to test all attributes to begin using a multimetric index; instead, they can build on studies that have been done before. Nevertheless, whenever more than five sites with different human influences can be sampled, we encourage testing of metric responses in particular locales to see whether the patterns observed elsewhere can be generalized.

Before building a multimetric index, you must convert metric data into a common scoring base. Typically, metrics are quantified with different units and have different absolute numerical values (e.g., numbers of taxa may range from 0 to a few dozen; relative abundances of certain groups may range from 0% to 100%). Also, some metrics increase in response to human disturbance (e.g., percentage of omnivores) while others decrease

Table 7. Potential metrics for benthic stream invertebrates. Metrics that responded to human-induced disturbance as predicted are indicated by a check (✓); those marked with a dash (—) were not tested. Percent sign (%) denotes relative abundance of individuals belonging to the listed taxon or group(s). Metrics marked with an asterisk (*) have been included in a 10-metric multiregional B-IBI (Karr 1998a; see also Table 11). Human influence in the Tennessee Valley consisted primarily of mining and agriculture; in southwestern Oregon, logging and road building; in north-central Oregon, altering riparian condition; in the Puget Sound lowlands, urbanization (measured by percentage of impervious surface); in Japan, multiple human influences; and in Wyoming, recreation.

Metric	Predicted response	Tenn. Valley	SW Ore.	NC Ore.	Puget Sound	Japan	NW Wyo.
Taxa richness and composition							
Total number of taxa*	Decrease	✓	✓		✓	✓	
Ephemeroptera taxa*	Decrease	✓	✓		✓	✓	✓
Plecoptera taxa*	Decrease	✓	✓	✓	✓		✓
Trichoptera taxa*	Decrease	✓	✓	✓	✓	✓	
Long-lived taxa*	Decrease	—	✓		✓	—	
Diptera taxa	Decrease						
Chironomidae taxa	Increase		—	—			
Tolerants and intolerants							
Intolerant taxa*	Decrease	✓	✓	✓	✓	✓	✓
Sediment-intolerant taxa	Decrease	✓ᵃ	✓	✓	—	—	—
% tolerant*	Increase	✓	✓		✓	✓	✓
% sediment-tolerant	increase	—	✓	✓	—	—	—
% planaria + amphipods	Increase	—	—	—	✓	—	—
% oligochaetes	Increase	✓				✓	
% chironomids	Increase						
% very tolerant	Increase	—	—	—	—	✓	
% "legless" organisms	Increase	—	—	—	—	✓	
Feeding and other habits							
% predators*	Decrease	✓		✓			✓
% scrapers	Variable	✓		✓			✓
% gatherers	Variable			✓			
% filterers	Variable	✓					
% omnivores	Increase	✓					
% shredders	Decrease			✓			✓
% mud burrowers	Increase	—	—	—	—	✓	✓
"Clinger" taxa richness*	Decrease	—	—	—	✓	✓	—
Population attributes							
Abundance	Variable	✓					✓
Dominance*	Increase	✓	✓			✓	✓

ᵃ Taxa richness at sediment surface

Table 8. Metrics used in the original fish index of biological integrity (IBI) for midwestern U.S. streams and equivalents for more general application.

Original fish IBI	General fish IBI[a]
Number of fish species	Number of native fish species
Number of darter species	Number of riffle-benthic insectivores
Number of sunfish species	Number of water column insectivores
Number of sucker species	Number of pool-benthic insectivores
Number of intolerant species	Number of intolerant species
Relative abundance of green sunfish	Relative abundance of individuals of tolerant species
Relative abundance of omnivores	Relative abundance of omnivores
Relative abundance of insectivorous cyprinids	Relative abundance of insectivores (specialized insectivores)
Relative abundance of top carnivores	Relative abundance of top carnivores
Number of individuals	*Not a reliable metric*
Relative abundance of hybrids	*Not often used successfully*
Relative abundance of diseased individuals	Relative abundance of diseased individuals

[a] Metrics chosen vary as a function of stream size, temperature class (warm-, cool-, cold-water), and ecological factors to reflect biogeographic and other patterns, including sensitivity to different human influences.

(e.g., overall taxa richness). To resolve such differences, each metric is assigned a score based on expectations for that metric at minimally disturbed site(s) for that region and stream size. Metrics that approximate what biologists would expect at minimally disturbed sites are assigned a score of 5; those that deviate somewhat from such sites receive a score of 3; those that deviate strongly are scored 1 (Karr 1981, 1991; Karr et al. 1986). The final index is the sum of all the metrics' scores (Figure 21).

In all cases, the basis for assigning scores is "reference condition," that is, the condition at sites able to support and maintain a balanced, integrated, and adaptive biological system having the full range of elements and processes expected for a region; thus IBI explicitly incorporates biogeographic variation into its assessment of biological condition. In some regions, biologists can actually find and sample from sites that have not been influenced, or have been influenced only minimally, by humans. In other regions, where pristine sites are unavailable, biologists may have to infer reference condition based on knowledge of the evolutionary and biogeographic processes operating in the region (see Premise 31). In still other cases (Fausch et al. 1984; Hughes 1995; Hughes et al. 1998), researchers must depend on historical data, collected when human activity was less, to define reference condition.

Simple, uniform rules for setting scoring criteria—the range of numerical

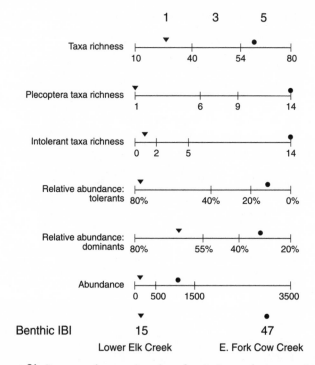

Figure 21. Range and numeric values for six invertebrate metrics from a severely disturbed site (lower Elk Creek, ▼) and a less disturbed site (East Fork Cow Creek, ●) in southwestern Oregon. Because the metrics have different quantitative values, they are given scores (5, 3, 1) to put them on the same scale: 5 indicates little or no deviation from expected, or reference, condition; 3 indicates moderate deviation from expected condition; and 1 indicates strong deviation from expected condition. Vertical lines in the figure represent the cutoff points for assigning these metric scores. Total benthic IBI (B-IBI) value for these two sites equals the sum of these metric scores and five others (from Fore et al. 1996).

values that qualify a metric for a score of 5, 3, or 1—are thus difficult to specify because they depend in part on the sampling design that generated the data. In a hypothetical watershed where one-third of sampled sites were pristine, one-third moderately disturbed, and one-third highly disturbed, the values for each metric could simply be divided at the 33d and 67th percentiles. But human activities tend to homogenize landscapes and living systems so that a majority of sites in a given watershed are likely to be moderately or even severely degraded, such as in the Japanese study illustrated in Figure 22. In the real world, therefore, it makes sense to err on the conservative side by expanding the middle score (3) or even the low score (1) to include more sites rather than fewer, thus making it more difficult for a site to attain a high score.

Natural shifts or breaks in the distribution of metric values can guide the setting of scoring criteria; indeed, scoring criteria should be adjusted to fall at these points, because the points often reflect a biological response. Where metric values increase or decrease linearly across the gradient of human influence (Figure 22, top), as in total taxa richness, the values are typically trisected into three equal divisions, each representing the criteria for assigning a score of 1, 3, or 5. Other metrics, such as relative abundance of

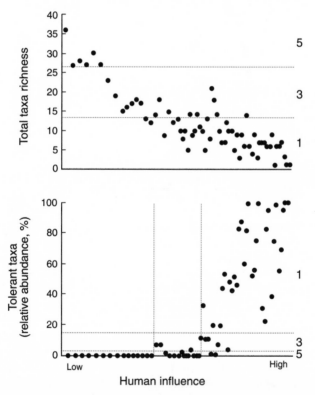

Figure 22. Plots of two sample metrics showing different ways to set the criteria for assigning metric scores of 1, 3, and 5. For metrics with a monotonic, or linear, distribution (e.g., total taxa richness: *top*), one divides into roughly equal thirds the range from 0 to the highest value. For metrics that are not distributed monotonically, one uses natural breaks in the distribution to define score boundaries (shown in the bottom plot by vertical dotted lines). Metric values and classification scheme for human influence come from Rossano (1995) (see also Figures 4 and 5).

tolerant organisms or particular trophic groups, respond in a more skewed pattern (Figure 22, bottom; Figure 23); for these metrics, natural break points suggest setting scoring criteria in unequal divisions. Setting scoring criteria is an iterative process and should be revisited as regional databases and biological knowledge expand.

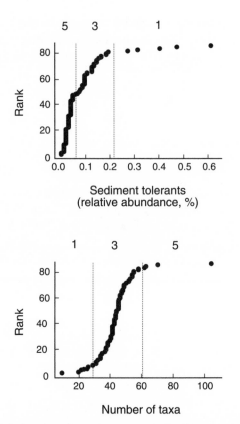

Figure 23. Relative abundance (percentage of sediment-tolerant individuals) and taxa richness (number of taxa) plotted against the rank order of that metric value for 86 stream sites sampled in southwestern Oregon. Dotted vertical lines mark the range of values (scoring criteria) for scoring metrics as 5, 3, or 1. Most sites have near 0% sediment-tolerant individuals; only very degraded sites show higher values of this metric. In other words, the distribution pattern for this metric is skewed. Taxa richness, in contrast, is less skewed. Scoring criteria are divided into unequal divisions for skewed metrics, reflecting a biological response in the data (*top*); the divisions are more equal for unskewed metrics (*bottom*). In both cases, most sites receive a score of 3, the most conservative interpretation of condition.

The statistical properties of multimetric indexes are known

Multimetric indexes are statistically versatile. We can use familiar statistical tests, such as *t*-tests or analysis of variance (ANOVA), to look for significant differences in index values because IBI satisfies the models' assumptions (Fore et al. 1994). In addition, because IBI is a single integrating number, it serves as a yardstick to rank (compare) sites according to their relative condition. Finally, from statistical power analysis, we know that an IBI formulated and developed as we propose can detect six distinct categories of resource condition (Fore et al. 1994; Doberstein et al., unpubl. manuscript). Because we know the statistical precision of a given IBI, we can use IBIs to discover and define differences among sites caused by changes through time or space.

Using bootstrap analysis[7] of fish data from Ohio, we determined that the distribution of IBI at one stream site is unimodal (Figure 24); integrating metric scores into a multimetric index thus allows us to take advantage of properties of the mean. Integration can be done by summing or averaging the metric scores; the results are equivalent. For the fish IBI, averaging metric scores reduced the variance and increased precision (Fore et al. 1994). The values for multimetric indexes approximate a normal distribution (Fore et al. 1994), probably because averages tend to be distributed normally by the central limit theorem (Cassella and Berger 1990); consequently, multimetric indexes can be tested with familiar statistics such as ANOVA or regression.

The IBI distribution satisfies the assumptions for ANOVA, even though the strong unimodal peak with no tails (expected given the way scores are calculated) is not strictly normal (see Figure 24). These assump-

---

[7] The bootstrap algorithm creates new samples by randomly selecting and replacing elements from the original sample. Random sampling with replacement continues until the bootstrap sample contains the same number of elements as the original sample. Many such samples are generated to approximate the distribution of IBI at a site.

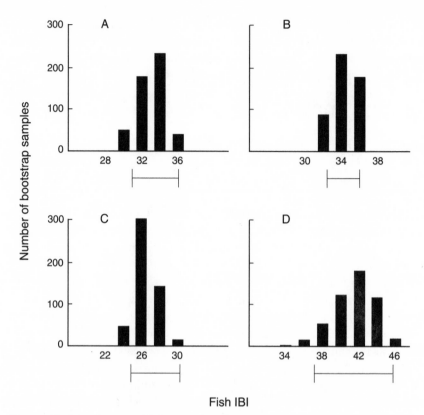

Fish IBI

Figure 24. Distribution of fish IBI values from bootstrapping analysis for four typical stream sites in Ohio; the unimodal distributions approximate a normal distribution. The line below each x-axis marks the 95% confidence interval (< 8). A difference of ± 4 points in IBI values therefore represents a statistically significant change in biological condition (from Fore et al. 1994).

tions for ANOVA are: (1) the error term is unbiased; (2) measurement error is not correlated among sites; (3) variance is homogeneous; and (4) the distribution of the error term is normal (assumed only for hypothesis testing).

Some regulatory situations require statistical evidence that a significant change has occurred in the field. The statistical properties of IBI make it an appropriate choice for these situations. In reality, however, management decisions are rarely based on the outcome of a statistical test or its associated p-value. Often, sites within an area need to be ranked so that funds for restoration can be allocated or so that policies to determine human use can be evaluated. Managers and policymakers therefore need to know something about the magnitude of differences across sites and, most important, whether observed differences are biologically meaningful. Without this kind of information, they cannot ascertain the causes of those differences.

A multimetric index provides a yardstick for measuring and communicating the biological condition of sites, but how many tick marks are on the yardstick? In other words, what is the precision of the index? On the basis of a statistical power analysis of fish data from Ohio EPA, IBI can detect six distinct categories of biological condition (Figure 25). Ohio EPA's version of IBI, like the original IBI, ranges from 12 to 60. For this index, 95% of the variability in IBIs generated by the bootstrap procedure fell within ±4 points of the observed IBI (Fore et al. 1994). These results confirmed previous estimates of confidence intervals based on field observations through time (Angermeier and Karr 1986; Karr et al. 1987).

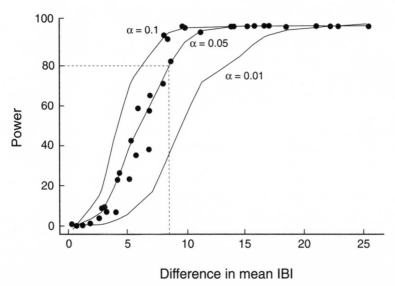

Difference in mean IBI

Figure 25. Power curves for the fish IBI estimated from nine locations sampled three times by the Ohio EPA (from Fore et al. 1994). Actual points are shown only for α = 0.05; other values of α are pictured as smoothed lines. For 80% power (a value accepted by most researchers), IBI can reliably detect a difference of about 8 points at an α-level of 0.05 (projected onto the x-axis, as indicated by dashed lines). Total IBI can range from 12 to 60, a difference of 48; thus IBI can detect six nonoverlapping categories of biological condition.

Multimetric indexes reflect biological responses to human activities

Human activities degrade water resources by altering one or more of five principal groups of attributes—water quality, habitat structure, flow regime, energy source, and biotic interactions—often through undetected yet potentially devastating effects on water resources (Table 9; Karr 1991, 1995b). Human activities such as logging, agriculture, and urbanization affect water quality by introducing sediment and raising water temperature (Bisson et al. 1992; Megahan et al. 1992; Gregory and Bisson 1997; Williams et al. 1997). Habitat structure changes when large woody debris is removed from a channel, or when sediment fills the spaces among cobbles. When vegetation is removed from a watershed, streams and rivers flood more heavily and more often, or they may dry up entirely. Logging of riparian areas also alters the energy sources in a stream: removing riparian vegetation removes one source of allochthonous organic material; disrupts entry of large woody debris to the channel; and also increases light reaching the stream, which in turn increases water temperature and algal growth and thus the algal material available to fish and invertebrates. Overfishing and introducing alien species, including native fish raised in hatcheries, alter relationships among predators and prey or competitors. As these changes stress and alter the normal assemblage of stream organisms, they degrade the stream.

Because multimetric indexes are sensitive to these five factors, they quantify the biological effects of a broad array of human activities. The effects of logging were generally reflected in benthic IBIs from southwestern Oregon (Figure 26), even though logging was quantified simply as the percentage of total watershed area that had been logged (Fore et al. 1996). Secondary influences on B-IBIs in these watersheds included road density and location. In east-central Illinois (Karr et al. 1986), fish IBIs revealed the influences of agriculture: IBIs were lowest at sites where cultivation reached

Table 9. Five features of water resources altered by the cumulative effects of human activity, with examples of degradation in Pacific Northwest watersheds (from Karr 1995b).

Attribute	Components	Degradation in Pacific Northwest watersheds
Water quality	Temperature, turbidity; dissolved oxygen; acidity; alkalinity; organic and inorganic chemicals; heavy metals; toxic substances	Increased temperature and turbidity Oxygen depletion Chemical contaminants
Habitat structure	Substrate type; water depth and current speed; spatial and temporal complexity of physical habitat	Sedimentation and loss of spawning gravel Obstructions interfering with movement of adult and juvenile salmonids Lack of coarse woody debris Destruction of riparian vegetation and overhanging banks Lack of deep ponds Altered abundance and distribution of constrained and unconstrained channel reaches
Flow regime	Water volume; flow timing	Lower low flows and higher high flows limiting survival of salmon and other aquatic organisms at various phases in their life cycles
Food (energy) source	Type, amount, and size of organic particles entering stream; seasonal pattern of energy availability	Altered supply of organic material from riparian corridor Reduced or unavailable nutrients from carcasses of adult salmon and lampreys after spawning
Biotic interactions	Competition; predation; disease; parasitism; mutualism	Increased predation on young by native and alien species Overharvest by sport and commercial fishers Genetic swamping by hatchery fish having low fitness Alien diseases and parasites from aquaculture, including hatcheries

streamside and stream channels had been dredged and straightened; IBIs were higher downstream, where the riparian area was left as either pasture or forest and the stream channel was intact (Figure 27). In the West, urbanization produced lower IBIs than logging did, and large cities (Seattle) yielded lower IBIs than small cities (Jackson, Wyoming) (Kleindl 1995; Fore et al. 1996; Patterson 1996; Karr 1998a).

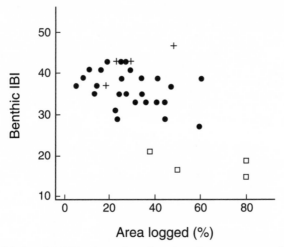

Figure 26. Benthic IBI values plotted against the percentage of area logged in watersheds in southwestern Oregon in 1990. Percentage of watershed area logged alone is an incomplete measure of human influence because information about type of logging, time since logging, or location and type of roads is not included. Nevertheless, B-IBI clearly distinguishes the best available (+) from the degraded (□) sites. (Compare Figure 12.)

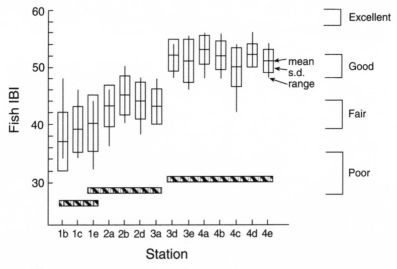

Figure 27. Fish IBI values for Jordan Creek, a first- to third-order stream in east-central Illinois (from Karr et al. 1986). Higher values represent changes in the fish assemblage that reflect improved biological conditions from stations 1 through 4.

Multimetric indexes can detect many influences in both time and space, reflecting changes in resident biological assemblages caused by single point sources, multiple point sources, and nonpoint sources. Biological monitoring of fishes in Chesapeake Bay watersheds revealed a variety of impacts from industrial, agricultural, and urban land uses (Hartwell 1997a; Hartwell et al. 1998). Fish assemblages were less diverse in urbanizing watersheds than in those dominated by forests and wetlands. A comparison of such biological results with a toxicological risk-ranking model using data from sediment and water column assays showed that the toxicological model could predict biological impacts only when chemical contamination was responsible. IBI or community diversity indexes revealed a wider range of biological impacts that the risk-ranking model could not pick up.

Multimetric indexes are useful in monitoring one watershed or several, and they permit comparisons over a wide geographic area. On the North Fork Holston River in Tennessee, for example, taxa richness of mayflies, stoneflies, and caddisflies (see Figure 18), as well as overall B-IBI (Figure 28), fell sharply immediately downstream of a streamside sludge pond (Kerans and Karr 1994). In another study across six midwestern regions or watersheds with different degrees of land development, fish IBIs differed markedly (Figure 29; Karr et al. 1986). Yet despite their different fish faunas, the regions could be compared on a single quantitative scale of biological condition.

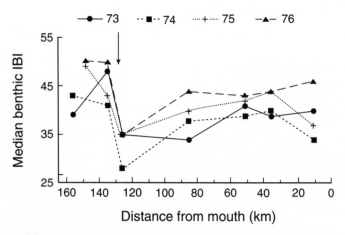

Figure 28. Median B-IBI values for the North Fork Holston River in the Tennessee Valley from 1973 to 1976 (from Kerans and Karr 1994). The arrow marks the location of a streamside sludge pond. (Compare Figure 18.)

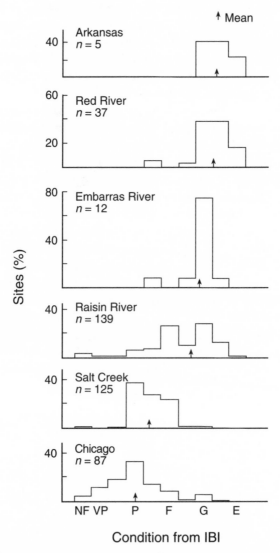

Figure 29. Distribution of sites in six midwestern regions or watersheds according to biological condition. The fish IBI was used to distinguish six categories of condition: NF, no fish; VP, very poor; P, poor; F, fair; G, good; and E, excellent. The IBI values varied across the six regions depending on the type and intensity of human land use (from Karr et al. 1986).

The wide-ranging responsiveness of multimetric biological indexes makes them an ideal tool for judging the effectiveness of management decisions. Along the Scioto River, Ohio, for example, fish IBI values for data collected in 1979 paralleled degradation caused by habitat deterioration and wastewater effluent (Figure 30). By 1991, after improvements in effluent treatment processes, IBI values had substantially increased; the benefits of management were clearly visible as higher IBIs along the river. Similarly, removal of a dam on the Milwaukee River, Wisconsin, improved physical in-stream habitat, raised the number of smallmouth bass, lowered the number of common carp, and raised fish IBIs (Kanehl et al. 1997). The numbers of tolerant species and omnivores went down while those of darters or suckers went up; the share of top carnivores and insectivorous minnows also rose. The rise in IBIs based on these metrics thus clearly showed the benefits of dam removal. Management actions may also decrease IBI. Upstream of a woodlot in Indiana, for example, a local effort to stabilize the channel

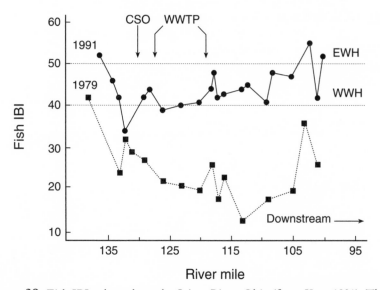

Figure 30. Fish IBI values along the Scioto River, Ohio (from Karr 1991). The lower IBIs reflect degradation associated with combined-sewer overflow (CSO) and wastewater treatment plants (WWTP). Improvements in effluent treatment, reflected in an overall increase in IBIs from 1979 to 1991, brought most of the sites into compliance for warm-water habitat (WWH); some sites even scored as excellent warm-water habitat (EWH).

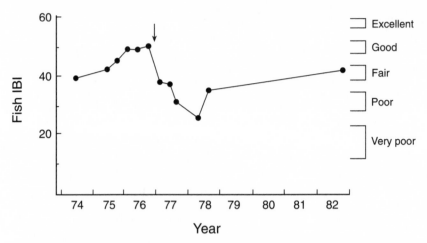

Figure 31. Changes in fish IBI values over time in Wertz Drain in Wertz Woods, Allen County, Indiana. During 1974–76, Wertz Drain had relatively high IBI values for a first-order stream in an area of intensive agriculture. The channel was sinuous, pools and riffles were well developed, and there were trees shading the channel. Although this site was not intentionally modified, a poorly executed bank stabilization project upstream during 1976 transported sediment to the site. Consequently, habitat quality deteriorated, as did the resident fish community. IBIs clearly trace the decline and slow improvement in stream condition over time.

transported substantial sediment into the woodlot reach and sharply lowered IBI (Figure 31). Graphs of IBI values in cases like these can be quickly and easily interpreted by policymakers and concerned citizens as well as by research biologists.

How biology and statistics are used is more important than taxon

The taxonomic group most appropriate for assessing environmental condition depends on the region to be assessed; agency resources; special staff expertise; and, most important, how biological knowledge is applied in designing sampling and analysis protocols (Karr 1991). Of the 47 states with bioassessment programs in place, 20 use fish, 44 use benthic invertebrates, and 4 use algae (periphyton or diatoms) (Davis et al. 1996). Twenty-six states use more than one major group, such as fish as well as invertebrates. No one taxon is correct or incorrect in a monitoring program. Like using 10 to 12 IBI metrics, sampling more than one taxon creates some redundancy. But in many circumstances, the redundancy pays off by substantially improving your ability to diagnose the causes of degradation, causes that may be apparent only if more than one assemblage is sampled (e.g., fish and invertebrates, fish and algae).

In the Pacific Northwest, benthic invertebrates have some advantages over fish as the primary subjects for biological monitoring (Fore et al. 1996). Macroinvertebrate taxa are numerous, ubiquitous, abundant, and relatively easy to sample; their responses to a wide spectrum of human activities are relatively easy to interpret. Moreover, because their life cycles extend several years, some benthic invertebrates are excellent integrators of past human influences. But fish also have advantages. Taxa such as sculpins, cyprinids, and suckers are often well represented in numbers of species and individuals in Pacific Northwest streams. Broadly ranging species such as anadromous salmonids offer a tool for monitoring large landscapes and the effects of harvest, hatcheries, and barriers to migration (R. M. Hughes, pers. commun.). Some biologists recommend including more than one vertebrate class (e.g., fish and amphibians) in any IBI based on vertebrates (e.g., Peter Moyle, cited in Miller et al. 1988; Hughes et al. 1998).

Convenience, money, time, or place will also affect the choice of taxon to sample. Chosen taxa should be cost-effective to collect and identify. Most fish (exceptions include some sculpins, minnows, and darters) can be identified at once in the field. More equipment may be required for fish (e.g., electrofishing gear) than for invertebrates, although both require more-complex equipment in deep-water environments. Permit requirements, too, may be more complicated for sampling fish than for sampling benthic invertebrates or algae. Insects and diatoms, on the other hand, are easier to sample in the field but more difficult and time consuming to identify in the laboratory.

Watershed size and location can affect the consistency of results obtained using different taxa. Assessments based on fish and invertebrates may disagree, depending on river size or region. In large watersheds (>500 square miles), for example, fish and benthic IBIs ranked sites the same only 44% of the time (Yoder and Rankin 1995a). The two kinds of IBIs gave the same results 65% of the time for midsize streams and rivers (50 to 500 square miles) and 75% of the time for small streams (Yoder and Rankin 1995a). According to R. M. Hughes (pers. commun.), species richnesses of fish and invertebrates rarely agree for Appalachian streams or New England lakes. A high-priority challenge is to determine if these apparent inconsistencies reflect real differences in the sensitivity of the different assemblages or if they result from differences in sampling effectiveness for fish and invertebrates as a function of water body size.

Finally, you have to be careful that taxa chosen for biological monitoring reflect real changes in the local and upstream landscape. The absence of anadromous fishes may not indicate that a site is in poor condition: a natural waterfall may simply be blocking fish passage, or their absence may reflect ocean conditions or overharvest rather than site condition. Migratory birds or fishes inhabiting estuaries or the ocean for part of their life cycles may be affected more by conditions elsewhere than by those in the monitored streams. Indeed, landscape-level factors may well have more effect on local and regional biological integrity than do traditionally monitored alterations in physical or chemical habitat (Richards et al. 1996, 1997; Roth et al., 1996; Allan et al. 1997; Koizumi and Matsumiya 1997; Wang et al. 1997; Hughes et al. 1998). Species listed as threatened or endangered under the Endangered Species Act provide an important signal about landscape conditions; including them in an IBI may even improve management of these species by putting them squarely into their larger biological context (Karr 1994).

In short, different taxa have different advantages for different places. As for all aspects of designing a biological monitoring program, researchers need to tease out the patterns of response among taxa from the artifacts of defining reference condition or of sampling itself; they need to consider carefully how different taxa might permit a better diagnosis of the causes of degradation in different geographic areas and situations. The most accurate assessments of biological condition may well come from determining biological condition using IBIs based on more than one assemblage.

Sampling protocols are well defined for fishes and invertebrates

The utility of any measure of biological condition in a stream depends on how accurately the original sample represents the biota present in that stream—that is, how successful it is in avoiding statistical "bias." Indeed, a fundamental assumption of the fish IBI is that the sample on which it is based reflects the taxa richness and relative abundances of the stream's fish, without bias toward taxa or size (Karr et al. 1986). Implicit in this assumption is that sampling effort is standardized. Any fish-sampling protocol must therefore be consistent, comprehensive, and representative of the stream's microhabitats, including pools, riffles, margins, and side channels. A study of fish of the Muese River in Belgium reinforced this point, revealing that sampling multiple mesohabitats (riffles, pools, and runs) was needed to accurately evaluate river quality (Didier and Kestemont 1996).

Many researchers have helped to refine the protocols for sampling fish to evaluate or implement an IBI (Ohio EPA 1988; Lyons 1992a,b; Lyons et al. 1995, 1996). Other protocols for sampling fish and invertebrates have also been described, although their goals and applications vary somewhat from development of an IBI (Klemm et al. 1990, 1993, for U.S. EPA's Environmental Monitoring and Assessment Program [EMAP]; Cuffney et al. 1993 and Meador et al. 1993 for U.S. Geological Survey's National Water Quality Assessment [NAWQA]).

Early work on the fish IBI identified sampling gear, the range of microhabitats in a stream, and stream size as important factors affecting sampling accuracy (Karr et al. 1986; Ohio EPA 1988). These researchers showed that, with standard procedures, it is feasible to sample virtually all fish from all microhabitats in small to medium-sized streams. Boat-mounted electrofishing gear is the most effective and most efficient in the widest variety of stream types. Early work by Angermeier and Karr (1986) suggested that fully sampling from two entire meanders typically captures the variety of stream microhabitats, yielding enough individual fish to calculate taxa richness and relative abundances for IBI metrics. Later work in several geographic areas suggests about 40 channel widths as the appropriate length of sampling efforts (Lyons 1992b; Angermeier and Smogor 1995; Paller 1995a,b). In relatively homogeneous systems (e.g., low-gradient streams), longer distances may be needed (Angermeier and Smogor 1995).

Large rivers, lakes, reservoirs, and coastal and estuarine environments contain diverse habitats. No single sampling method is appropriate to every one of those habitats, yet using multiple sampling methods is difficult, expensive, and thus impractical. So, selective sampling protocols, which measure biological condition on the basis of one or a few local microhabitats, have been developed for these systems (Thoma 1990; Weaver et al. 1993; Jennings et al. 1995; Deegan et al. 1997; Whittier et al. 1997b; Whittier 1998).

Benthic invertebrates, such as insects, crayfish, and worms, pose different sampling challenges: more species to deal with than among fishes, more microhabitats, more sampling techniques and protocols appropriate for the variety of microhabitats. Therefore, you must either use many different protocols to get a representative invertebrate sample or first test whether sampling from a single microhabitat accurately represents stream condition.

In their study of streams in the Tennessee Valley, Kerans et al. (1992) sampled invertebrates from pools (Hess sampler) and riffles (Surber sampler) and evaluated 18 invertebrate attributes as indicators of human influence. They concluded that monitoring designs "that quantitatively sample multiple habitats, are spatially replicated, and use many different attributes for assessment provide a good method for determining biological condition" (Kerans et al. 1992: 388). Although a number of invertebrate attributes behaved similarly for pools and riffles, others (e.g., mayfly taxa richness, caddisfly taxa richness) matched expected stream health rankings better for pools than for riffles. When the researchers combined metrics to create a B-IBI, patterns were stronger for pools than for riffles. Rankings were not always consistent for pool and riffle data (Kerans and Karr 1994), perhaps because these studies were done in relatively large rivers with substantial sedimentation, which might be detected more readily in pool environments (B. L. Kerans, pers. commun.).

Debate still rages over whether single- or multiple-habitat sampling is best with invertebrates. Some contend that a single habitat is adequate; others insist that sampling multiple habitats is essential. Our experience suggests that sampling a single habitat is appropriate and adequate, although our reasons for this conclusion do not always agree with others'. Sampling riffles, for example, is often justified on the grounds that riffles are the most diverse, the most productive, or the dominant habitat (Plafkin et al. 1989;

Barbour et al. 1996b, in press). We are not convinced that these claims are true or even at issue. Still, because we have successfully and cost-effectively used single-habitat samples to discern human effects on small streams (Kerans et al. 1992; Kerans and Karr 1994; Kleindl 1995; Rossano 1995, 1996; Patterson 1996), we recommend a single-habitat sampling protocol that concentrates on riffles.

Because a Surber sampler samples only part of a riffle, a single sample may not be precise enough to judge stream condition. We therefore tested the effects of replicate sampling of invertebrates, using data from the John Day River basin of north-central Oregon (Fore et al., unpubl. manuscript). Five replicates were collected, and their contents were identified for each of seven sites (Tait et al. 1994). Using a bootstrap resampling algorithm, Fore et al. simulated the effects of taking one, three, or five replicates at a site. Fore et al. changed the number of replicates for each site to test whether metric precision varied as a function of the number of replicates (Figure 32). With only one replicate, a metric could either increase or decrease depending on which of the five replicates was chosen by the bootstrap algorithm. In practice, therefore, the numerical value of a metric calculated using a single Surber sample at a site would depend on where in the riffle that sample had been taken. When the mean of three replicates is plotted, however, the relationship between metric scores and human influence is more consistent (see Figure 32). Metric precision increases little if five replicates are collected instead of three. Thus we conclude that the increased costs of sample collection and analysis for three replicates over one are justified, but not those for five replicates.

For invertebrates, therefore, we recommend a standard sampling area of approximately 0.1 square meter (a Surber sampler frame of 0.3 meters by 0.3 meters) and three replicate samples for each site. We also recommend collecting from riffles for three reasons: (1) riffles are easier to define and identify by field crews than are pools or margins; (2) riffles are more uniform than other stream microenvironments and thus easier to compare across watersheds; and (3) riffles are shallow, and the current through them is fast, making sampling with kicknets or Surber samplers easier. We also take all replicates in a single riffle; this strategy characterizes one site more fully than does the alternative of sampling once in each of several riffles, as some protocols propose (e.g., EMAP; R. M. Hughes, pers. commun.).

These methods work well in small to midsized streams. For large rivers—where Surber and similar methods are difficult to use, or it is necessary to minimize the effect of habitat differences among sampling sites—

Figure 32. Results of bootstrapping analysis (random sampling with replacement) of the relative abundance (percentage) of predators for seven stream sites along a gradient of riparian condition in the John Day Basin, Oregon. For each site, one, three, or five replicates were randomly selected, and least-fit regression lines (100 in each graph) were plotted. The lines in the upper graph are based on means for one replicate (out of five possible) per site; in the middle, for three replicates per site; in the bottom graph, for five replicates per site. Precision increases with number of replicates, especially between one and three replicates; in fact, the relationship between site condition and proportion of predators may appear either negative or positive with only one replicate. Note, however, that precision increases relatively little from three to five replicates. The lower two graphs clearly show that the relative abundance of predators increases as resource condition improves.

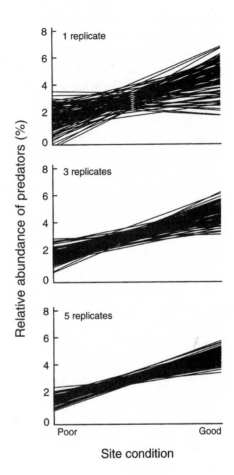

sampling with artificial substrates, such as the Dendy samplers used by Ohio EPA, may be preferable (Cao et al. 1996).

It is especially important to collect and count a sufficient number of insects to characterize the biota in multiple dimensions. If sampling fails to yield a total of 500 or more organisms (for example, in regions where natural invertebrate densities are low), the number of replicates or the sampled area may need to be increased. We believe that sampling enough organisms is far more important than how sampling is organized (e.g., single or multiple riffles, composite samples, or no composite samples). Subsampling that counts only 100, 200, or even 300 organisms, as recommended by RBP and some other protocols, tends to reduce the utility of many metrics that have become standard in multimetric assessments (Doberstein et al., unpubl. manuscript; see Premise 29).

It is not always necessary to identify insects to species; strong patterns emerge from samples where most insects are identified only to genus (except for chironomids). Identification to genus provides distinct advantages over identification only to family, however—in particular, by strengthening the ability to discriminate among sites of intermediate quality (Figure 33). In

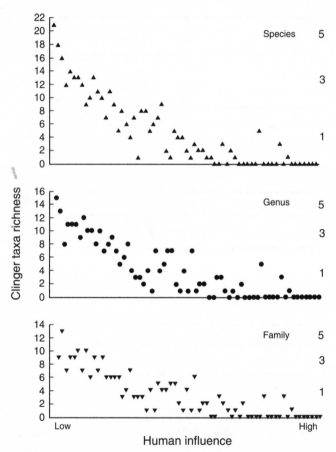

Figure 33. Number of clinger taxa present in samples of benthic invertebrates from 65 Japanese streams ranked according to intensity of human influence (see Figures 5 and 6). The pattern is consistent across the influence gradient, regardless of the level of taxonomic identification, but the slope becomes smaller from species to genus to family, reducing the metric's usefulness for discriminating among sites at higher taxonomic levels. (Data provided by E. M. Rossano.)

California coastal marine environments, for example, family identifications were optimal for detecting the effects of organic pollution on benthic taxa richness, dominance, and diversity (Ferraro and Cole 1990, 1995).

Using standard methods for sampling invertebrates (Box 2), we have been able to detect changes in biological condition caused by a whole range of human influences from the Grand Tetons (Patterson 1996) to streams in several areas of Oregon and Washington (Kleindl 1995; Karr, Morley, and Adams, unpublished data).

Finally, for both fishes and invertebrates, timing of sampling is important. Karr et al. (1986) recommended periods of low to moderate stream flow for sampling fishes. For benthic invertebrates, recent experience leads us to recommend late summer, before autumn rains begin. We sample stream insects in the Pacific Northwest in September. Water flows are generally stable and safe for field work at that time of year, and invertebrates are abundant. Sampling at this time also minimizes disturbance to the redds, or nests, of anadromous fish. Optimal sampling period will, of course, vary regionally and should be set on the basis of knowledge of the regional biota, precipitation patterns, and other relevant factors.

Box 2. How to sample benthic invertebrates.

Equipment
  Modified 500-micron Surber sampler with cod end (receptacle)
  2.5-gallon bucket (dishpan works well too)
  Squirt or spray bottle
  Forceps
  Marking tape
  500-micron soil sieve
  Sample jars (8-ounce or 4-ounce; 4-ounce urine specimen bottles are an
    inexpensive alternative)
  Plastic sandwich bags (Ziploc) for loose lids
  Pure ethanol; diluted by sample to about 70%
  Permanent markers (Sharpies)
  Pencils
  2 white, deep-sided sorting pans for large debris
  Small rake, trowel, or other implement (e.g., piece of rebar or old screwdriver) with
    marking tape at 10 centimeters
  50-meter measuring tape
  Flagging
  Stopwatch
  Camera to photograph site and surrounding environment
  Kitchen spatula for transferring material from sieve to sample jar
  Pocket knife (always handy)
  Spares of selected items above

(continues)

Selecting a Sample Reach

The choice of a stream reach to sample should be guided by a study's specific aims and by watershed characteristics. But sampling for biological monitoring must never lose sight of the ultimate goal: to detect and measure human influence in watersheds. Factors to consider include stream size, stream gradient, range of microhabitats in the reach, and length of sample reach.

Selecting a Sample Site

The distribution of invertebrates in small streams is patchy, driven by associations among the animals and stream microhabitats (e.g., riffles, pools, and raceways, or erosional and depositional areas). For that reason, our standard protocol calls for collecting three replicate samples as follows:

1. Sample in the "best" natural riffle segment within a study reach, even if doing so does not give an exact match of substrates for all study streams. Sediment types may vary among streams, especially in association with different human activities within watersheds. Ideal sampling substrates consist of rocks 5 to 10 centimeters in diameter sitting on top of pebbles. Avoid substrates dominated by rocks larger than 50 centimeters in diameter.
2. Sample within the stream's main flow.
3. Sample at water depths of 10 to 40 centimeters.
4. Collect three replicate samples in a single riffle; depth, flow, and substrate type should be similar for the three replicates.
5. Begin sampling at the downstream end of the riffle and proceed upstream to collect the three replicates; avoid the transition zone from the riffle to a downstream pool or other habitat.

Sampling the Site

Sampling teams may consist of two to four people. Collecting the macroinvertebrates requires two people; others can assist with equipment, labeling, taking notes, and other tasks. Sample as follows:

1. Place the Surber sampler on the streambed with the opening of the nylon net facing upstream. Brace the brass frame and hold it firmly on the substrate, especially on the side attached to the net to prevent invertebrates from slipping under the net.
2. While one person holds the brass frame under water, the other person should lift any large rocks within the frame and wash into the stream any organisms crawling or loosely attached to the rocks, so that the organisms drift into the nylon net. Put the washed rocks into a bucket for further picking on shore.
3. When large rocks have been removed, cleaned, and placed in the bucket, thoroughly stir the remaining substrate with the rake or trowel. Stir to a depth of 10 centimeters for a short period (about one minute) to loosen organisms in the interstitial spaces and to wash them into the net. If you find more large rocks with organisms on them, wash the organisms into the net and put the rocks into the bucket.
4. Now slowly lift the brass frame off the substrate, tilting the net up and out of the water. Use the water's flow to wash trapped or clinging organisms into the Surber sampler's cod end.
5. Carry the net and the bucket to shore for picking or for transferring to alcohol to sort, count, and identify in the lab. The Surber sampler's

removable receptacle makes the transfer relatively simple. Use the squirt bottle to wash down the sides of the net before removing the cod end. Using the magnifying glass and forceps, collect and preserve every organism from the Surber sampler as well as from the rocks and water in the bucket. After removing the cod end, wash its contents through the soil sieve, picking out large rocks, detritus, and other debris for hand sorting. Transfer any organic matter remaining on the sieve to sample jars, taking care not to damage invertebrates. A plastic kitchen spatula and squirt bottle work well to dislodge clingers from the sides of the net or the sieve.

6. Put a pencil-on-paper label into each sample jar and label the outside with permanent ink; include the date, sample location (name and number), and replicate number.

7. Rinse the net *thoroughly* after each sample to avoid cross-contamination.

When to Sample

Species composition and population sizes of macroinvertebrates vary substantially through a river's seasonal cycles. Because the goal is to assess the influence of human actions, not natural variation through time, collect samples during a short period. For Pacific Northwest streams, late summer or early autumn is best. This timing gives representative samples of stream invertebrates and simultaneously:

1. Avoids endangering field crews (as in seasons of high water).
2. Standardizes seasonal context.
3. Maximizes efficiency of the sampling method because flows are neither too high nor too low.
4. Avoids periods when flows are likely to be too variable.

In the Pacific Northwest, we sample in September, before the autumn rains begin. Shifting the sample period a bit earlier into August or extending it into October is acceptable. But all samples should be collected within a period of not more than four weeks.

(For a 20-minute video of this sampling protocol, contact Global Rivers Environmental Education Network at greennw@econet.org or (360) 676-8255.)

The precision of sampling protocols can be estimated by evaluating the components of variance

Calculating components of variance is a simple and useful technique for estimating the relative contribution of measurement error and site differences to the overall variance of a metric or index. In general, our goal is to select metrics that have small measurement error relative to the differences we want to measure—changes related to human activities.

For example, we used zooplankton data from northeastern lakes studied under EPA's EMAP to estimate the relative contribution of three sources of variability to the overall variance observed for each of three metrics: taxa richness, relative abundance, and density (Hughes et al. 1993; Stemberger and Lazorchak 1994; Stemberger et al. 1996). In that study, one to three zooplankton samples were collected from each of seven lakes. The data were then subsampled in the laboratory and the organisms taxonomically identified. In our analysis, we identified three sources of variability, and thus three components of variance in those data: variability caused by differences among lakes (lake effects), variability caused by differences in sample location within the lake (crew error), and variability caused by different subsamples identified in the lab (lab error). These three sources of variance for metric scores can be summarized in an ANOVA model as:

$$\text{Metric score} = \text{lake}_i + \text{crew error}_{j(i)} + \text{lab error}_{k(ij)}$$

where lake_i = the effect of the ith lake on metric score; $\text{crew error}_{j(i)}$ = the variability caused by crew differences, sampling time, or location within the ith lake; and $\text{lab error}_{k(ij)}$ = the variability that arises from the laboratory subsampling protocol used in the initial study.

In statistical language, this model is a two-level nested ANOVA that is unbalanced because the number of replicates varies at each level. Using the sums of squares from the computer output and a little algebra (Sokal and Rohlf 1981: Chapter 10), you can estimate the variance of each term in the model.

For this analysis, we assumed that the lakes differed in human influence and thus biological condition. We were interested in how the lakes differed from one another. We were not interested in evaluating differences within lakes or within subsamples; therefore, these two sources of variability were considered sources of error. A variable is typically labeled an "effect" when you want to measure or compare values for that variable; if, on the other hand, you do not care whether crew A collects more animals than crew B ("crew effects"), for example, then you seek to avoid that source of variability altogether, and so it is labeled "error."

Based on our analysis of the components of variance in the zooplankton samples (Figure 34), we concluded that the sampling protocol was adequate to detect lake differences when taxa richness or relative abundance were calculated. We also discovered that lab variability was relatively small and that using lab time to identify replicate samples was not necessary. In contrast, metrics varied relatively more depending on where in the lake crews collected samples. Consequently, we recommend that future studies like this one should put more effort into sampling from the lakes while reducing the number of lab subsamples.

We arrived at another important conclusion by comparing taxa richness, relative abundance, and density. The error components of variance for density were much larger than the lake component; for density, any signal at the lake level was lost in the noise of variability. In contrast, for taxa richness or relative abundance, most of the variability occurred among lakes rather than among replicate samples and subsamples (see Figure 34). If the goal is to distinguish among lakes, then you should select metrics that minimize variability caused by within-lake and within-lab differences and maximize variability resulting from human influence. Taxa richness and relative abundance are metrics that do so.

We analyzed components of variance in two other locations—the Puget Sound lowlands and Grand Teton National Park vicinity, Wyoming—to compare the sources of variance with total variance in benthic IBIs for homogeneous sets of streams (Figure 35). Rather than looking at individual metrics, these studies focused on the indexes themselves, *after* individual metrics had been tested and integrated. For samples within riffles in Puget Sound lowland streams, approximately 9% of the total variance in B-IBI

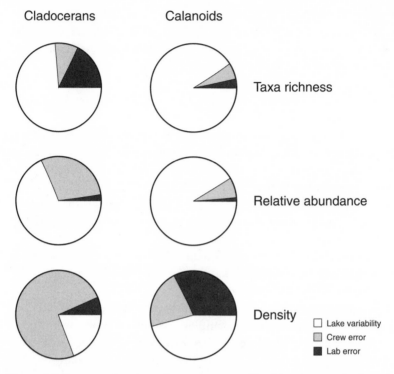

Cladocerans   Calanoids

Taxa richness

Relative abundance

Density
☐ Lake variability
▨ Crew error
■ Lab error

Figure 34. Sources of variance for two groups of herbivorous zooplankton (clado-cera, such as *Daphnia*, and calanoid copepods), calculated for northeastern lakes (using data collected by R. S. Stemberger under EPA's Environmental Monitoring and Assessment Program). Taxa richness, relative abundance of individuals, and density were calculated for each group. The lab protocol used to subsample ("lab error") and replicate samples taken from each lake ("crew error") constituted two sources of error; differences from lake to lake ("lake variability") were the effect of interest. Number of lakes, 7; number of crew replicates, 1–3; number of lab repli-cates, 1–3. Components of variance were estimated with ANOVA.

arose from differences within streams (Figure 35, top). (For this study, human influence was measured as a continuous variable, the percentage of impervious area; see Figure 7.)

The Grand Teton study did not measure human influence in each watershed. Instead, all sampled streams were assigned to one of four cate-gories of human influence, and variance was apportioned according to its source: among members of a group or among groups. B-IBI differences

Puget Sound lowlands

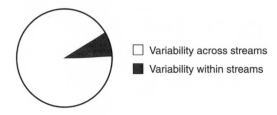

Grand Teton National Park

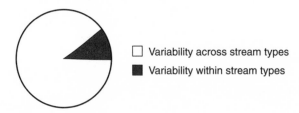

Figure 35. Components of variance for the B-IBIs for sites ($n = 30$) in the Puget Sound lowlands and ($n = 16$) in or near Grand Teton National Park, Wyoming. In Puget Sound, variability associated with stream differences was large relative to variability associated with microhabitat (within-riffle) differences. In Wyoming, variability associated with different categories of streams (grouped according to land use) was much higher than variability associated with streams within each group. Components of variance were estimated with ANOVA.

among members of the groups contributed 11% to the overall variance in B-IBI. Eighty-nine percent of the variance came from differences among the groups that reflected discrete human influence classes: little or no human activity; light recreational use; heavy recreational use; and urbanization, grazing, agriculture, or wastewater discharge (see Figure 8). In the Puget Sound and Grand Teton studies, the sources of error were low relative to variance resulting from different types of human land use.

Statistical analysis of metric and index variance is thus useful for tuning sampling protocols; it is important in defining where to put your efforts and in determining the usefulness of an index to detect human effects. But it cannot take the place of the more important aspects of testing and analysis that link metric and index values to human influence. The most desirable statistical properties are no substitute for a biologically meaningful dose-response relationship to human disturbance.

Multimetric indexes are biologically meaningful

A multimetric IBI for a site is a single numeric value, but one that includes the numeric values of individual indicators of biological condition. The actual measured values of the component metrics—each metric deliberately chosen because it represents a specific biological part or process that changes reliably as human influence increases—are not lost when an IBI is calculated. An IBI itself, along with patterns in the component metrics, focuses attention on biologically meaningful signals. Each numeric metric value, and the IBI as well, can be translated into words for a variety of audiences, including nonscientists, enabling them to understand immediately how the biology at high-scoring sites differs from that at medium- or low-scoring sites. Each metric and IBI value thus translates into a verbal and visual portrait of biological condition.

A site labeled "excellent" on the basis of a fish IBI, for example, is comparable to the best streams without human influence (Karr 1981). A full complement of species expected for the habitat and stream size is present, including the most sensitive or intolerant forms. (Note that not all regionally distributed species will be found at any single sampling site; even the best sites contain only a fraction of regional species.) In addition, long-lived taxa are present in the full range of age and size classes; the distribution of individuals and taxa indicates a healthy food web with a balanced trophic structure or organization. In contrast, a fair-quality site has very few sensitive or intolerant forms and a skewed trophic structure (e.g., larger numbers of omnivores and relatively few top predators, especially in older age classes). At a very poor site, few fishes are present, except for introduced or tolerant forms, and more than a few individual fish are likely to show deformities, lesions, or tumors. Similar descriptions can convey the details of biological condition for benthic invertebrate assemblages. In contrast, the ecological context of many chemical criteria, bioassays, and biomarkers is often unclear.

The combination of numeric and narrative descriptions that come from a multimetric IBI makes communication possible with virtually all academic disciplines, stakeholders, and communities. The opportunity for education is thus part and parcel of a multimetric approach.

Multimetric protocols can work in environments other than streams

The principles for developing sampling protocols and analytical procedures for monitoring running waters are broadly applicable to other environments. Substantial progress was made in applying these principles to aquatic environments in the 1990s, and work in terrestrial environments is beginning:

- *Lakes:* Weaver et al. 1993; Larsen et al. 1994; Minns et al. 1994; Pinel-Alloul et al. 1996; Stemberger et al. 1996; Gerritsen and White 1997; Whittier et al. 1997a,b; Carpenter et al. 1998; Harig and Bain 1998; Jennings et al. 1998; Whittier 1998; Wildhaber and Smith 1998

- *Freshwater wetlands:* Adamus 1996; Carlisle et al. 1998; Danielson 1998; Karr 1998c; Mensing et al., in press; U.S. EPA 1998

- *Riparian systems:* Brooks and Hughes 1988; Croonquist and Brooks 1991; Spackman and Hughes 1995

- *Reservoirs:* Jennings et al. 1995; McDonough and Hickman 1998

- *Coastal and marine systems:* Ferraro et al. 1989, 1991, 1994; Nelson 1990; Deegan et al. 1993, 1997; Engle et al. 1994; Weaver and Deegan 1996; Deegan et al. 1997; Ferraro and Cole 1997; Hartwell 1997a,b; Hartwell et al. 1997, 1998; Kennedy 1997; Thoma and Yoder 1997a,b

- *Terrestrial systems:* Karr 1987; van Swaay 1990; Erhardt and Thomas 1991; Kremen 1992; Holl and Cairns 1994; Holl 1995, 1996; Blair 1996, 1998; Andersen 1997; Blair and Launer 1997; Ferretti 1997; Stohlgren et al. 1997; Bradford et al. 1998; Nelson and Epstein 1998

Some agencies have recognized the potential of multimetric biological indexes to help achieve regulatory, management, and restoration goals.

Arguing that strong biological monitoring and assessment must be cost-effective, scientifically and legally defensible, integrated with existing management programs, and communicated effectively, the Florida Department of Environmental Protection has begun applying multimetric approaches to lakes, wetlands, southern Florida canals, and coastal and estuarine systems (McCarron and Frydenborg 1997). Such efforts are changing the management framework for water resource protection.

Freshwater lakes. Applying IBI principles to lakes has taken place more slowly than for streams for a variety of scaling, sampling, and perceptual reasons (Weaver et al. 1993; Whittier 1998), but the pace is picking up. On the more theoretical side, Carpenter et al. (1998) stress the importance of looking at the effects of contrasting land uses—essentially a gradient of human influence—on watersheds. They suggest that management decisions should be seen as experiments to be tracked for what they can tell us about the dynamics of these systems. They continue to concentrate, however, on nutrient enrichment, particularly phosphorus enrichment from nonpoint sources, rather than on how human activities affect the other five factors important to the condition of aquatic systems (see Premise 17).

Harig and Bain (1998), in contrast, explore the application of multimetric biological assessment to the restoration of biological integrity to wilderness lakes in the Adirondack Mountains of New York. After an exhaustive review of lake ecology, these investigators chose nine metrics for testing, including dominance of native fish, dominant phytoplankton taxa, and number of zooplankton species. Their conclusion: "Ecosystem-scale indicators of biological integrity in lakes are powerful tools for identifying disturbance, providing target conditions for ecosystem recovery, and identifying disturbed lakes."

Freshwater wetlands. Wetlands have been the center of government and citizen attention for decades. Under the Clean Water Act, the federal government's policy is supposedly "no net loss," yet the nation has already lost more than half its wetlands to dredging and filling for navigation and development. Most wetland assessment and conservation efforts have concentrated on documenting the "functions" and "values" of wetlands. Little emphasis has been placed on overall wetland condition until recently, as state agencies and EPA take more interest in "wetland bioassessment" (Danielson 1998; U.S. EPA 1998).

Wetland assessments follow two main approaches: a hydrogeomorphic, functional assessment approach for classifying and assessing wetlands (Brinson 1993; Brinson and Reinhardt 1996) and multimetric evaluations of biological condition (Danielson 1998; U.S. EPA 1998). Multimetric methods are being developed in more than 12 states, stretching from Florida and Massachusetts across the northern prairie (North Dakota, Minnesota) to the West (Montana, Wyoming, Washington). Testing metrics is advanced in many of those states. Promising metrics cover varied taxa, including insects, algae and other plants, birds, reptiles, and amphibians.

Coastal and marine systems. Thanks in part to the terms of the Magnuson-Stevens Fishery Conservation and Management Act, which require the National Marine Fisheries Service (NMFS) to assess "habitat quality" for some 600 fish species, interest in biological monitoring of coastal marine and estuarine waters is growing (Hartwell 1997a,b). Ohio EPA is also developing multimetric tools for "lacustuaries," where streams enter Lake Erie (Thoma and Yoder 1997a,b). Fish are being used in multimetric approaches in Massachusetts, Chesapeake Bay, North Carolina, Florida, and Texas. Invertebrates are being assessed in mid-Atlantic states south and west to the Gulf of Mexico and in Washington. Metrics with ecological relevance are being sought for benthic, pelagic, and vegetated habitats from tidal creeks and small estuaries to water bodies the size of Chesapeake Bay. Participants in a workshop devoted to this topic have urged NMFS to develop and test metrics for the following habitats: submerged aquatic vegetation, riparian areas, estuarine benthic and pelagic zones, coastal benthic habitats, and coral reefs.

Although they have not built a multimetric index per se, studies of marine benthic organisms typically use multiple measures of biological condition such as taxa richness, dominance, and degree of tolerance to detect organic effluent (Ferraro et al. 1989, 1991, 1994) or sediment contamination by DDT (Ferraro and Cole 1997).

Terrestrial systems. Applying multimetric concepts to terrestrial environments has so far been limited. In contrast to work in aquatic systems, most efforts to examine biological condition in terrestrial environments have focused on threatened or endangered species or on local and regional biodiversity (Stevens 1998). There has been less emphasis on understanding and documenting broader biological responses to human influence, and most relevant studies have examined individual biological attributes rather than a set of metrics.

In one early study, species richness declined with declining size of forest fragments (Williamson 1981). In midwestern agricultural landscapes, the relative abundance of omnivorous birds increased as the size of forest frag-

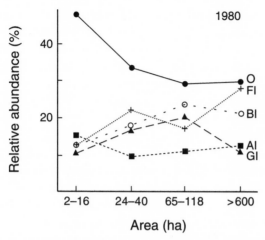

Figure 36. Percentage of individuals in several trophic groups among birds of forest islands in east-central Illinois: O, omnivores; FI, foliage insectivores; BI, bark insectivores; AI, aerial insectivores; and GI, ground insectivores. The relative abundance of omnivores increases as size of the forest fragment decreases; relative abundances of the other groups do not change as systematically.

ments fell; other feeding groups did not change systematically with fragment size (Figure 36; Karr 1987).

In a mist-net study of tropical forest birds, Karr (1987) detected disturbance-associated shifts in species composition, capture rates, and trophic organization within the undergrowth assemblage. Species richness in standard samples declined by 26%, and capture rates doubled, in a disturbed forest relative to an undisturbed forest; in this case, the disturbance was a recent history of intensive research within the forest. Although the number of species changed little in the major foraging guilds, spiderhunters, which feed on insects and nectar, increased sharply with a change in undergrowth plants in the disturbed area.

Butterflies and moths (lepidopterans) have been widely used as ecological indicators because they often associate with specific food and reproductive host plants (van Swaay 1990; Kremen 1992; Holl and Cairns 1994; Holl 1995, 1996; Nelson and Epstein 1998). They appear to be particularly sensitive to degradation, sometimes revealing disturbance even before the effects can be detected in the host plant population (Erhardt and Thomas 1991). The connection between butterflies and other arthropods and their host plants may also provide signals about the success of restoration programs (Holl 1995, 1996). "Restored" sites may look green, but they may not in fact have their full complement of plant and lepidopteran species (Holl and Cairns 1994). The presence of a few common butterfly species may mask fundamental changes in biological condition that would be revealed by tracking rarer species. Such studies demonstrate the need to keep in mind that broader biological condition is the primary monitoring endpoint.

Relatively few terrestrial studies have examined multiple dimensions of biological change along a continuum of human influence. One exception is work by Blair (Blair 1996, 1998; Blair and Launer 1997) in Santa Clara County, California. Blair studied both birds and butterflies along a gradient comprising an urban reserve, a golf course, a residential neighborhood, and a business district. The species richness of birds declined across this gradient, and invasive and alien taxa increased. Butterflies characteristic of pre-development areas disappeared as sites became more urban. Blair concluded that shifts in habitat structure brought shifts in species composition according to the animals' life histories and patterns of resource use.

Ferretti (1997) also uses multiple attributes of forests to evaluate what he calls forest ecosystem health (analogous to our use of the word *integrity;* see Premise 4), forest health (the condition of a population of trees), and tree health (the vigor of individual trees). His indicators of the ecological condition of oak forests in Italy include foliage chemistry, pest and disease intensity, soil biota, species composition at different forest levels, litterfall, nutrient turnover rates, estimated biomass for various taxa, and animal abundance.

In 1996, Karr et al. (1997) began developing the first full-scale IBI for a terrestrial locale, the Hanford Nuclear Reservation in eastern Washington State. Under the jurisdiction of the U.S. Department of Energy since 1943 for weapons production, the 560-square-mile reservation was closed to public access and development for more than half a century. As a result, Hanford is a paradox. On the one hand, it poses an enormous toxic-cleanup challenge to the Department of Energy, whose Office of Environmental Management has been at it since 1989; on the other, the reservation and its surroundings comprise some of the state's largest contiguous patches of native shrub-steppe vegetation and the last spawning run of chinook salmon in the mainstem Columbia River. The vegetation before European settlement consisted of shrubs (*Artemisia* spp., *Chrysothamnus* spp., and *Purshia tridentata*) and perennial bunchgrasses (*Agropyron spicatum, Festuca idahoensis, Stipa* spp., and *Poa* spp.). The number of alien annual plants increased with increasing human activity (Daubenmire 1970; Rickard and Sauer 1982), persisting even long after the activity ceased. The abundance of insect taxa shifted after wildfires (Rogers et al. 1988).

The Hanford area is ideal for testing potential metrics for an IBI because it presents a full array of kinds and degrees of human impact. Initial field work established 13 study sites across this gradient, including agricultural lands and lands altered by heavy equipment, fire, and grazing (Figure 37). A site was also chosen from the neighboring Arid Lands Ecology Reserve (ALE), which has been minimally disturbed. Plants and

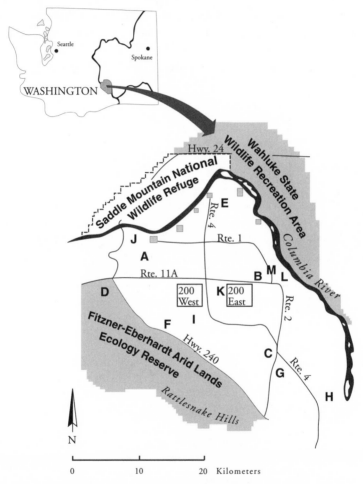

Figure 37. The Hanford Nuclear Reservation, including central Hanford, the Arid Lands Ecology Reserve (ALE), Wahluke State Wildlife Recreation Area, and Saddle Mountain National Wildlife Refuge. Letters indicate location of study plots. Sites C, G, and H have been affected by fire; site D by an early history of grazing; sites J and M by agriculture; and sites F, K, and L by physical disturbances. Sites A, B, and D show only minimal disturbance (reference sites). Sites E and I have unknown disturbance histories.

insects were the two organismal groups chosen for metric testing and IBI development.

Altogether 58 plant species, representing 20 families, have been found from the 13 sites; 72% of these are native and 16% are introduced aliens. The distribution of particular species (e.g., the alien cheatgrass *Bromus tectorum* and native grasses) and the proportion of native vs. alien species varies across the sites. The proportion of alien species per site ranges from 28% to 92%; it is highest at the most disturbed sites. The percentage of alien species and the percentages of native grass and shrub taxa may offer potential plant metrics (Figure 38).

On the basis of insects from 4 of the 13 sites, taxa richness appears to be

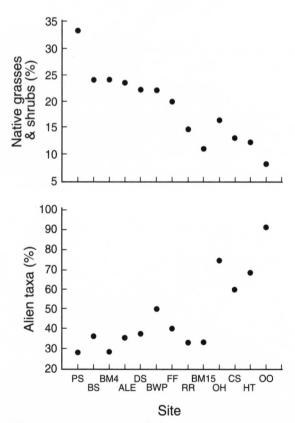

Figure 38. Preliminary ecological dose-response curves for two potential metrics for plants at 13 Hanford sites: *top*, relative abundance of native shrubs and grasses (percentage of total), and *bottom*, relative abundance of alien species.

higher at the minimally disturbed ALE site (49 insect families) than at the old town of Hanford (29 families), a burn site (23 families), or an abandoned agricultural field (23 families) (Figure 39). Relative abundances also vary across these sites. A common agricultural pest (cutworm, a noctuid moth) made up 89% of the lepidopterans at an abandoned agricultural site, but no species dominated among the butterflies and moths at the other sites. Beetles, especially one species (*Eusattus muricatus,* family Tenebrionidae), dominate at the burn site but not at the others. Other promising attributes include the number of predators and parasitoids; food web effects that may show up as shifts in species composition from site to site; and the numbers, taxa richness, and taxa composition of bees, wasps, and ants (hymenopterans). Hymenopterans are particularly interesting because they occupy a wide range of trophic levels. At the old town site, an area dominated by the alien yellow star thistle (*Centaurea solstitialis*), hymenopterans had the highest relative abundance (38%) of the insects collected there. Perhaps a link exists between hymenopteran pollinators and the introduced weed, an interaction that may offer a useful metric.

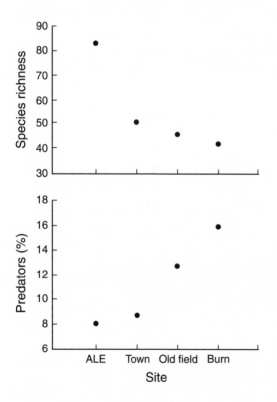

Figure 39. Preliminary ecological dose-response curves for two potential metrics for insects at four Hanford sites: *top*, species richness, and *bottom*, relative abundance of predators (%).

Section IV

For a Robust Multimetric Index, Avoid Common Pitfalls

Rigorously constructed multimetric indexes are robust measurement tools, although their development and use can sometimes be derailed. The failure of a monitoring protocol to assess environmental condition accurately or to protect running waters—or any other environment—usually stems from conceptual, sampling, or analytical pitfalls. Multimetric indexes can be combined with other tools for measuring the condition of ecological systems in ways that enhance or hinder their effectiveness. Like any tool, they can be misused. That multimetric indexes can be, and are, misused does not mean that the multimetric approach itself is useless.

For best results, avoid these pitfalls:

Conceptual
- Excessive dependence on theory

- Narrow conceptual framework

- Failure to account for a gradient of human influence

- Expectation of simple chemical (or other) correlations

- Poor definition or misuse of reference condition

Sampling
- Inadequate design

- Too many or too few data

- Misunderstanding of the sources of variability

- Failure to sample across a gradient of human influence
- Inappropriate use of probability-based sampling

Analytical
- Use of incompatible data sets
- Failure to keep track of sources of variability
- Failure to understand cumulative ecological dose-response curves
- Inattention to important signals, such as rare species
- Failure to test metrics

Properly classifying
sites is key

Successful biological monitoring depends on judicious classification of sites. Yet excessive emphasis on classification, or inappropriate classification, can impede development of cost-effective and sensible monitoring programs. Using too few classes fails to recognize important distinctions among places; using too many classes unnecessarily complicates development of biocriteria. Inappropriate levels of classification also lead to problems. The challenge is to create a system with only as many classes as are needed to represent the range of relevant biological variation in a region and the level appropriate for detecting and describing the biological effects of human activity in that place.

Like a taxonomy of places, classification attempts to distinguish and group distinct environments, communities, or ecosystem types; the proper approach to classification may vary, however, according to specific goals. For aquatic systems, biological (community) classification generally lags far behind classification by physical environment or habitat type (Angermeier and Schlosser 1995). The characteristics that make streams similar or different biologically—and thus make classification important for biological monitoring—are determined first by the geophysical setting (including climate, elevation, and stream size), and second by the natural biogeographic processes operating in a place (see Premise 6 and Figure 4). Together these are responsible for local and regional biotas. Coastal rainforest headwaters on the Olympic Peninsula, for example, are likely to be biologically comparable, as would be headwater streams in central Illinois.

But even though geophysical context is a fundamental determinant of variation in biological systems, classification based on the geomorphologists' view of stream channel types, or on other landforms occupied by biological systems, is not necessarily the proper level for assessing the biological condition of those systems. In the Pacific Northwest, geomorphologists identify some 50 to 60 channel types based on the interplay of physical and chemical processes that shape stream channels (MacDonald et al. 1991). But recognizing these channel types does not necessarily mean that an equal number of biological classes is needed for biological monitoring. The native biota may not be unique to each of those channel types in terms of species composition, taxa richness, or other important aspects of ecological organization; even if some species replacement occurs, metric norms may not change. Fewer biological categories may therefore work just as well.

Many agency programs rely on geographically delineated ecological regions reflecting prevailing geophysical and climatic regimes (Omernik 1995; Omernik and Bailey 1997). Such ecoregion divisions are valuable, but they are not the be-all and end-all of classification schemes. Indeed, classification at the ecoregion level alone is unlikely to give appropriate weight to every factor important to creating homogeneous sets for comparing the biological condition of streams. Other factors, including topography, geological substrate, and stream size or gradient may be more significant biologically. For example, in the Snake River, Idaho (Maret et al. 1997), and in Kansas streams (Hawkes et al. 1986), neither the distribution of fish species nor that of ecologically defined assemblages coincided with ecoregion boundaries.

In addition to ecoregion, a good classification scheme should consider the defining characteristics of local and regional physical and biological systems. It would make little biological sense, for example, to group large, meandering stream reaches with small, fast-flowing streams even if they are in the same lowland ecoregion; the habitats these stream reaches provide, and therefore the biota that live there, are very different. Likewise, the biological attributes signaling the effects of human activities in two high-elevation first-order streams may not differ just because they are in different ecoregions. In short, ecoregions (or equivalent units) are a useful but not a sufficient basis for a stream classification used in biological monitoring.

Characterizing ecoregions can certainly be valuable, but no matter how much such characterization enhances our knowledge of natural landscape variation, it should not get in the way of testing and using metrics diagnostic of human impact. The point of classification is to group places where the biology is similar in the absence of human disturbance and where the responses are similar after human disturbance. In some cases, these groupings may coincide with ecoregion boundaries; in others, they may cross those boundaries. To evaluate sites over time and place, we need groupings that will give reliable metrics and accurate criteria for scoring metrics to represent biological condition (see Premise 15).

On the east and west sides of the Cascades, and elsewhere in the Northwest, for example, many of the same metrics respond to the effects of grazing, logging, and urbanization, even though climate, vegetation, terrain, and human land use differ (Table 10). The expected values of these metrics differ—taxa richness, for example, is lower east of the Cascades—which may result from "natural" differences or differences stemming from more widespread human influence on a more fragile eastside landscape. Nevertheless, in both westside and eastside ecoregions, the same metrics respond across a range of human influence, and IBIs composed of these metrics reflect and distinguish among the effects at different sites. Elsewhere, such as across eastern deciduous forests and midwestern prairies, maximum species richness also transcends ecoregion boundaries (Figure 40). Expected species richness seems to be higher for forested landscapes than for prairie or grassland landscapes. Other metrics, such as trophic structure, however, are reliable indicators of human influence across ecoregions for some places and taxa (e.g., North American fishes) but not for others (e.g., benthic invertebrates) (see Premise 13).

Table 10. Similar metrics emerge as reliable indicators of human influence across the Pacific Northwest, regardless of ecoregion. Percent sign (%) denotes relative abundance of individuals belonging to the listed taxon or group. Metrics marked with a check are those that responded across a range of intensity for grazing (north-central Oregon and Wyoming) or logging (western Oregon and Idaho).

Metric	Predicted response	NC Oregon	SW Oregon	Central Idaho	NW Wyoming
Taxa richness and composition					
Total number of taxa	Decrease	✓	✓		✓
Ephemeroptera taxa	Decrease		✓	✓	✓
Plecoptera taxa	Decrease	✓	✓	✓	✓
Trichoptera taxa	Decrease	✓	✓		
Tolerants and intolerants					
Intolerant taxa	Decrease	✓	✓	✓	
Sediment-intolerant taxa	Decrease	✓	✓		✓
% tolerant	Increase		✓	✓	
% sediment-tolerant	Increase	✓	✓		
Feeding and other habits					
% predators	Decrease	✓		✓	✓
% scrapers	Variable	✓		✓	✓
% gatherers	Variable	✓		✓	
Population attributes					
Dominance	Increase		✓		

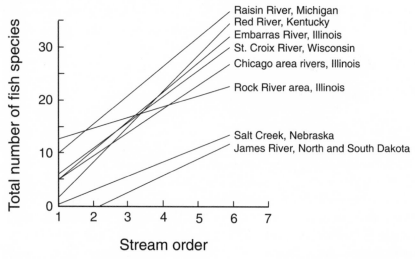

Figure 40. Lines of maximum species richness for stream order, based on historical data from midwestern streams. Although the lines differ for the eight watersheds, they fall into two general groups: woodland watersheds in several ecoregions in the eastern Midwest (upper group) and two Great Plains streams in two different ecoregions (after Fausch et al. 1984).

   Thus, classification based on ecological dogma, on strictly chemical or physical criteria, or even on the logical biogeographical factors used to define ecoregions is not necessarily sufficient for biological monitoring. The good biologist uses the best natural history, biogeographic, and analytical resources available to choose a classification system.

Avoid focusing
primarily on species

Many water quality specialists begin their analyses of stream data with a matrix of species and abundances. Using species-level community comparisons such as similarity indexes, Pinkham and Pearson's B, the Bray-Curtis index, or multivariate statistics, they then evaluate species overlap among sites and classify the sites based on these evaluations. Unfortunately, the mathematical and ecological properties of these measures (Wolda 1981; Washington 1984; Reynoldson and Metcalfe-Smith 1992) make them problematic. Because, like diversity indexes, similarity indexes are strongly influenced by patterns of disturbance and the initial structure of communities (Boyle et al. 1990; see also Premise 5), the results they yield are often ambiguous.

In a study of sites in the Thames and Trent River basins of England, Cao et al. (1997) tested nine similarity measures, including Jaccard, Sorenson, Bray-Curtis, Canberra, Morishita, and Horn. Not one of the nine indexes consistently grouped replicate samples from the same site together as more similar to one another than to samples from other sites; in other words, the indexes failed to discriminate among sites. Neither did the indexes consistently group all the samples from the same river together; that is, they failed to discriminate between rivers. The mathematical structure of each index weighted different factors affecting species composition differently, thus leading to different outcomes. Frustrated, Cao and colleagues developed a new community similarity-dissimilarity measure for benthic macroinvertebrates. But as long as the focus remains limited to species—species diversity or species overlap—the problems will persist.

Higher-level taxonomic and ecological structure usually provides better guidelines for classification. Consider two hypothetical undisturbed streams in adjacent Appalachian watersheds (Figure 41). A standard sample from a first-order stream in one watershed contains eight fish species: darters A, B, and C; sunfish D and E; and minnows F, G, and H. The other site contains seven species: darters M, N, and O; sunfish P and Q; and minnows R and S. Comparing the samples using measures of species overlap (0%) would high-

Site 1	Site 2
Before disturbance	
Darter A	Darter M
Darter B	Darter N
Darter C	Darter O
Sunfish D	Sunfish P
Sunfish E	Sunfish Q
Minnow F	Minnow R
Minnow G	Minnow S
Minnow H	
After disturbance	
Darter A	Darter M
Darter J	Darter J
Sunfish D	Sunfish D
Sunfish L	Sunfish P
Minnow F	Minnow R
Minnow K	Minnow K

Figure 41. Species composition for two hypothetical fish assemblages before and after a human disturbance that changes the biological condition of the sites. The lack of overlap in species composition before disturbance is not sufficient reason to conclude that these sites should be classified differently, for their ecological organization before and after disturbance is the same.

light the completely different species composition at the two sites, even though the higher-level taxonomic or ecological overlap (near 100%) is obvious at the family level and in feeding ecology. Both sites support three darters, two sunfish, and either two or three minnows.

Consider now what might happen after a disturbance at each site: the species composition of both streams shifts as another regional darter, J (a tolerant species), moves in, and two of the original darter species disappear from each stream because they cannot tolerate the changes caused by the disturbance. Similar changes occur in the other taxa (see Figure 41). Now the species overlap index for the two sites is more similar (33%), and both are less similar to their original assemblages (27% and 30%). Real assemblages with very different species composition respond in much the same way, becoming more similar in the presence of similar human activity. These responses result from their nearly identical ecological structure, not from similarities in species composition. It is this ecological structure that gives the clearest signals of human disturbance.

Thus ecological organization and regional natural history are better guides for site classification and for signaling human disturbance than a focus on species composition.

Measuring the wrong things sidetracks biological monitoring

A bewildering variety of biological attributes can be measured, but only a few provide useful signals about the impact of human activities on local and regional biological systems. Some attributes vary little or not at all (e.g., the number of scales on the lateral line of a particular fish species); others vary substantially (e.g., weight, which can vary with age and reproductive or environmental conditions). Variation may be natural or human induced, and natural variation may come from temporal (diurnal, seasonal, annual) sources, spatial sources (stream size, channel type), or both. Biological monitoring must separate human effects from natural variation by discovering, testing, and using those biological attributes that can be precisely measured to provide reliable information about biological condition.

Some attributes are poor candidates for monitoring metrics because of their underlying biology. In particular, abundance, density, and production vary too much to use in multimetric biological indexes (see Figures 19 and 34), even when human influence is minimal. These attributes, especially production, may also be very difficult to measure. Estimated density or species abundance at a site is affected by three sources of variance: sampling efficiency, natural events, and human activities (see Premise 20).

Population size can vary enormously even when conditions are stable (Botkin 1990; Bisson et al. 1992) because populations respond to natural environmental changes as well as to intrinsic dynamics such as lag times between developmental stages. Identifying correlates of population variation in natural environments is challenging enough, but where human influence is also at work, the complex interaction of human and natural events determining population size makes it almost impossible to separate human effects from sampling and natural variation. Sampling protocols have been developed to overcome this problem (see Premise 5; Schmitt and Osenberg 1996), but they are often complicated, expensive, and time consuming. Moreover, they may even fail to detect biological signals that can be detected by looking at other components of biological systems or by organizing and framing data in other ways. Taxa richness and relative abundance are more effective as indicators of biological responses to human actions (see Premise 5; Premise 13; Premise 14; Premise 20).

Some attributes, such as ratios (e.g., of the abundances of two trophic groups), are inherently flawed. A ratio consists of measures pertaining to two different groups, one used as the numerator, the other as the denominator. The numerator, denominator, or both may vary simultaneously and for diverse reasons. For example, a pair of very large numbers of scrapers and filterers may yield the same ratio as a pair of very small numbers of scrapers and filterers. Metrics expressed as ratios may intuitively seem useful, but empirical evidence (Barbour et al. 1992; Hannaford and Resh 1995; Fore et al. 1996) and statistical theory (Sokal and Rohlf 1981) show that when two variables are combined in a ratio, the ratio tends to have a higher variance than either variable alone. Moreover, if two attributes of an assemblage are potentially important, they should be evaluated independently. Using ratios mixes independent parameters in ways that make it hard to discern their relative influence, much as diversity indexes combine species richness and evenness into a single expression.

Not to be confused with ratios are metrics expressed as proportions (e.g., proportion of darters out of total number of individuals). The relative abundance, percentage, or proportion of a particular group is calculated as the number of individuals in that group divided by the total number of individuals present. That proportion changes only as the abundance of the target taxon changes. As the number of individuals in a sample becomes very small, however, such as in seriously impaired systems or systems with very few plant nutrients (highly oligotrophic), low numbers may distort proportions, and assessment procedures may need altering (e.g., Ohio EPA 1988).

Finally, many attributes now in use are based on theoretical arguments that often lack adequate empirical support. Although theory can be a good guide for selecting metrics, the theory must be tested with real-world data before a metric is used. Empirical natural history patterns should always take precedence over ecological theory in choosing which metrics to incorporate into a multimetric index. Theory can suggest metrics, especially when one begins to look at a new geographic region or a new biota. But the belief that a metric *should* work is not enough reason to conclude that it will. Ecology's path as a scientific discipline is littered with the carcasses of "good" theoretical constructs that evidence later showed were flawed. We should not rely on theory to guide decisions about vital goods and services that come from natural systems. Once again, the key test is whether an attribute shows an empirical dose-response relationship across a gradient of human influence.

Field work is more valuable than geographic information systems

Although a geographic information system (GIS) can be a powerful tool for mapping satellite and other data, it is not required for a successful monitoring project. The time and money spent on this technique may be better spent doing field work to identify the types and levels of human influence and defining the criteria for selecting and ranking sites.

Local field work leads to understanding and to decisions based on practical local experience with natural systems, on knowledge of the major human activities associated with those systems, and on the resulting biological responses. The most successful projects are those that identify major human land uses in a region and study existing information before sampling. GIS can be useful for managing and displaying information, but GIS technology is not a substitute, or even a good surrogate, for biological monitoring.

Sampling everything is not the goal

Biological systems are complex and unstable in space and time (Botkin 1990; Pimm 1991; Huston 1994; Hilborn and Mangel 1997), and biologists often feel compelled to study all components of this variation. Complex sampling programs proliferate. But every study need not explore everything. Biologists should avoid the temptation to sample all the unique habitats and phenomena that make biology so interesting. Managers, especially, must concentrate on the central components of a clearly defined research or management agenda—detecting and measuring the influence of human activities on a biological system.

Sites should be selected for sampling that are typical of a region and reasonably homogeneous with respect to important biogeographic features. Special habitat types—such as streams that are spring fed, ephemeral, or very large—may represent important and fascinating gaps in our biological knowledge, but if they represent a small percentage of a region's sites, they should be left out of broad surveys (unless, of course, they are the target of a particular monitoring program).

Biologists are trained to focus on the unique because unique environments often yield new insights into how biological systems operate. But for monitoring, it is more important to focus widely on changes caused by humans and to document those effects. The goal is not to measure every biological attribute; indeed, doing so is impossible. Rather, the goal is, first, to identify those biological attributes that respond reliably to human activities, are minimally affected by natural variation, and are cost-effective to measure; and, second, to combine them into a regionally appropriate index.

Putting probability-based sampling before defining metrics is a mistake

The purpose of biological monitoring is to measure the condition of places. Some practitioners insist that monitoring must begin with a probability-based, or random, sampling design to ensure that estimates of resource condition are statistically reliable (Larsen 1997; Olsen et al., in press). We argue that it is more important to first identify the biological attributes, or metrics, that give the clearest signals of resource condition—in other words, to first establish dose-response relationships to human activity. Starting with a random-sampling design before understanding which biological signals you need to measure is a mistake.

Random sampling may not permit development of an integrative IBI to measure human effects: random sampling can even make it difficult to discover patterns caused by human activities. Random sampling of sites does not guarantee that selected sites are homogeneous enough (properly classified) to be considered together. Neither does it guarantee that a full range of ecological states, from heavily degraded to undisturbed, will be studied. In fact, because human influence is so pervasive, most sites within a watershed are likely to be moderately to severely degraded; probability-based sampling is likely to miss the best and worst places if they are rare. Yet the best and worst sites are key for demonstrating biological responses to human influence, for developing and testing new metrics, and for calibrating scoring criteria (5, 3, or 1). By the same token, numerous studies demonstrate that subjective selection of reference sites can also be misleading (Patterson 1996; R. M. Hughes, pers. commun.; see also Premise 31).

Another drawback of probability-based sampling may be the cost of identifying every potential sampling site before a random sample can be selected. Perhaps most important, if an agency commits exclusively to this sampling design before determining the biological responses likely to give the most useful signal about resource condition, considerable money and time can be lost. The problem is most acute if the sampling design is short-circuited by a failure to gain access to sites on private lands. Finally, many institutions and agencies may lack the resources for sampling sufficient numbers of sites to apply probability-based surveys.

On the other hand, if we already have robust indicators, probability-based sampling is critical to evaluate the condition of a wide area if it is impossible to sample all the region's water bodies. Whenever probability-based sampling has been combined with strong indicators in recent years, degradation has been found to be more pervasive than originally believed. Probability-based sampling can also help avoid problems with a monitoring strategy that defines sites on the basis of known sources of degradation: a random sample can find sites that were omitted because their causes of degradation were unknown.

Three early steps are crucial to a robust monitoring protocol: first, classifying regional biological systems at appropriate levels—neither too detailed nor too superficial (see Premise 23); second, discovering biological patterns associated with human actions—the documentation of ecological dose-response curves (see Premise 6); and third, cross-checking to ensure that the classification system selected is appropriate for the data set (see Premise 23). Narrowly conceived and implemented probability-based sampling designs too often overlook one (or more) of these three steps, and can thus fail to detect biological patterns associated with human-induced degradation. The failure of some state and federal programs in the past decade can be traced to the failure to define metrics that exhibit dose-response curves before monitoring began.

Nevertheless, when classification and ecological dose-response are appropriately established in concert with probability-based sampling, the result can be especially useful because it allows biologists to make statistically defensible conclusions beyond the sampled sites. For riverine fish, for example, probability-based sampling can help to estimate the condition of rivers over a large region where the fish metrics and a fish IBI have already been tested and validated. For now, probability-based sampling is less useful with other taxonomic groups, such as zooplankton, ants, plants, and to some extent benthic invertebrates, because tests of metrics—the search for ecological dose-response curves—are incomplete for these groups.

Finally, probability based sampling makes little sense if you are interested in the condition of only one or a few sites, as a local watershed group might be. In this case, you don't need a random sample; rather, as always, you need to sample the biological attributes that give the clearest signals about the site's condition.

Counting 100-individual subsamples yields too few data for multimetric assessment

A number of sampling protocols have been used in multimetric biomonitoring. Although there are no absolute standards for sampling design or analytical technique, certain protocols are more effective than others in avoiding the pitfalls of too few data or poor-quality data.

Since the fish IBI was first developed in 1981, fish-sampling protocols have called for sampling all microhabitats within stream reaches from 100 meters to 1 kilometer long, depending on stream size. Fish IBIs have been developed for Ohio (Ohio EPA 1988; Yoder and Rankin 1995a,b), Wisconsin (Lyons 1992a; Lyons et al. 1996), Oregon (Hughes and Gammon 1987; Hughes et al. 1998), Canada (Steedman 1988; Minns et al. 1994), Mexico (Lyons et al. 1995), Europe (Oberdorff and Hughes 1992; Didier and Kestemont 1996), and elsewhere (Hughes and Oberdorff 1998). Sampling design has not been controversial, largely because standard sampling methods are effective at sampling most fish in most microhabitats in small to midsize streams.

One study dealing with the effects that sample size (number of individuals per sample) has on fish IBIs found that small samples were correlated with high measurement error; that is, the confidence intervals for IBIs increased as sample size decreased (Fore et al. 1994). Among 37 sites in Ohio's Great Miami Basin, 29 had confidence intervals for IBI of six or less (Fore et al. 1994; Figure 42). Seven out of 8 of the sites with confidence intervals greater than six had fewer than 400 individuals per sample. The loss of

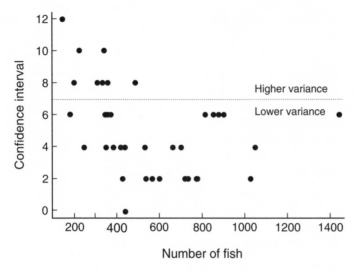

Figure 42. Confidence intervals for a fish IBI in relation to the number of individuals in samples collected at 37 sites within the Great Miami Basin, Ohio (from Fore et al. 1994).

precision in estimating IBI with samples of 400 or fewer suggests that it is unwise to intentionally use still smaller samples or subsamples.[8]

Sampling protocols are not as broadly accepted for benthic invertebrates as for fish. At least three superficially similar multimetric indexes using benthic invertebrates have been proposed: the invertebrate community index (ICI: Ohio EPA 1988; Yoder and Rankin 1995a,b); the rapid bioassessment protocol III (RBP: Plafkin et al. 1989); and the benthic index of biological integrity (B-IBI: Karr and Kerans 1992; Kerans et al. 1992; Kerans and Karr 1994; Fore et al. 1996; Rossano 1996; Karr 1998a). Both ICI and B-IBI were extensively tested before publication or use in research or management. For RBP, neither the sampling methods nor the metrics were evaluated as carefully, although recent tests are helping strengthen the protocol (Barbour et al. 1992; Barbour et al. 1996a, in press). Tests of B-IBI in several regions

---

[8] When small sample sizes are a result of severe degradation, scoring of metrics—especially for relative abundance—can be adjusted to account for this fact (Ohio EPA 1988). Researchers sponsored by EPA's Environmental Monitoring and Assessment Program for Oregon streams and rivers were able to get precise results with samples of as few as 100–200 fish (R. M. Hughes, pers. commun.). Perhaps the threshold varies in cold- vs. warm-water streams, an issue that deserves further exploration.

(Tennessee, Wyoming, Oregon, Washington, Japan) point to 10 metrics as appropriate for including in a broadly applicable B-IBI (Table 11).

One of the most controversial aspects of these three invertebrate indexes is the number of individual organisms to be counted for an analysis. Both ICI and B-IBI call for counting every individual in each sample. RBP, in contrast, calls for subsampling as few as 100 individuals from each large sample to define a "consistent unit of effort"; the adequacy of this number has been hotly debated (Fore et al. 1994; Barbour and Gerritsen 1996; Courtemanch 1996; Vinson and Hawkins 1996). The need for subsampling with RBP comes out of its initial design: RBP calls for sampling an area of 2 to 3 square meters "to integrate sampling among a wide range of heterogeneous microhabitats" (Barbour and Gerritsen 1996: 387). A smaller sampling area, such as 0.1 square meter, would reduce the heterogeneity among sampled microhabitats from the outset (Kerans et al. 1992; see Premise 19).

Table II. Ten-metric B-IBI based on study in six geographic regions. Metrics were tested in six benthic invertebrate studies done in the Tennessee Valley, southwestern Oregon, north-central Oregon, the Puget Sound region, Japan, and northwestern Wyoming. A + indicates that the metric varied systematically across a gradient of human impact for that data set; – indicates that the metric did not vary systematically; 0 indicates that the metric was not tested for that data set. Sources: Tennessee, Kerans and Karr 1994; southwestern Oregon, Fore et al. 1996; north-central Oregon, Fore et al., unpubl. manuscript; Puget Sound, Kleindl 1995; Japan, Rossano 1995; northwestern Wyoming, Patterson 1996.

Metric	Predicted response	Tenn. Valley	SW Ore.	NC Ore.	Puget Sound	Japan	NW Wyo.
Taxa richness and composition							
Total number of taxa	Decrease	+	+	+	+	+	+
Ephemeroptera taxa	Decrease	+	+	–	+	+	+
Plecoptera taxa	Decrease	+	+	+	+	–	+
Trichoptera taxa	Decrease	+	+	+	+	+	+
Long-lived taxa	Decrease	0	+	+	+	0	0
Tolerants and intolerants							
Intolerant taxa	Decrease	+	+	+	+	+	+
% tolerant	Increase	+	+	–	+	+	+
Feeding and other habits							
% predators	Decrease	+	–	+	+	–	+
"Clinger" taxa richness	Decrease	0	0	0	+	+	0
Population attributes							
% dominance (three taxa)	Increase	+	+	–	–	–	+

We have found unconvincing on several grounds one effort to justify the adequacy of the 100-individual subsample approach (Barbour and Gerritsen 1996), particularly with regard to studies of streams. First, the authors base their conclusions on data from lakes, not streams, and we believe it is not a good idea to extrapolate results across environment types. Second, arthropods were collected in "12 petite Ponar grabs (0.02 square meter)," giving a total sample area of only 0.24 square meter, in comparison with RBP's recommended 2–3 square meters for streams. Third, only one subsample was generated for each of nine sites; variation was assessed, not with multiple samples from a site, but from multiple sites. Nine sites were grouped according to relative abundance curves, creating a mathematical near certainty that taxa richness would vary systematically across the groups. A better approach would have been to examine sites of different known human influence, to construct multiple random samples from each site, and to examine if the ranking of sites or other inferences about the sites' relative condition (e.g., ability of different metrics to discriminate among sites) was influenced by the subsampling procedure.

The decision to count only 100-individual subsamples (intended to speed laboratory analysis) has serious ramifications for the counts' reliability in multimetric indexes. First, the counting procedure itself becomes a source of error or bias. In RBP, the samples are spread out in a sorting pan with a sampling grid, and grid squares are counted at random until 100 individuals have been counted. The initial process to "randomly distribute" the organisms is one potential source of bias. Bias also arises from differences in the identity, size, mass, density, or distribution of individuals among the squares; these attributes can influence results even if random selection of grid squares is strictly enforced.

In addition, sample size affects estimates of taxa richness and relative abundances, which are central to a robust multimetric index (Courtemanch 1996). Samples must be large enough to reflect the species richness and relative abundances accurately for the resident biota. Yet, argues Courtemanch (1996: 382–383), the 100-individual subsample does not provide an "asymptotic estimate," either of taxa richness (number of taxa per standard number of individuals) or of taxa density (taxa per standard area) in each sampled unit; thus "there is no basis for comparison with either another sample community or with a reference condition."

Courtemanch proposes two remedies for this problem: two-phase processing, in which the entire sample is first searched for large individuals belonging to rare taxa; and serial processing, which involves following the RBP procedure to count individuals in grids up to 100 and then counting more grids until no new taxa are found. The large-individual standard is appealing but, we find, hard to defend on either sampling or biological grounds (see also Walsh 1997). A similar approach is outlined by Vinson and Hawkins (1996).

It may be more efficient to sample a smaller, entirely "countable" area in the first place, rather than spending the time and effort to collect large numbers of organisms that are never counted. The protocol we recommend (see Box 2)

- Samples smaller areas

- Samples single microhabitat

- Collects three replicate samples

- Keeps samples separate

- Counts each sample completely

Such a protocol saves some time in the field and gives more-complete results from the laboratory; we thus have greater confidence in both the statistical and biological aspects of the resulting multimetric evaluation. This approach does not, of course, give a complete count of all organisms present in a stream reach or measure variation among riffles within the reach. It has, however, provided enough detail to judge relative biological condition among streams—within a region and among regions.

Perhaps the most serious flaw in the 100-individual subsample approach derives from the fact that sample size does not affect all metrics in the same way. Counting only 100 individuals may thus lead to erroneous conclusions or limit a manager's ability to diagnose causes of degradation. In testing the 100-individual standard, for example, Barbour and Gerritsen (1996) found that, for taxa richness, counting 100-individual subsamples and also counting all individuals produced the same rank order for their nine sample sites; they therefore concluded that 100 individuals adequately rep-resented taxa richness across these sites. Yet because these researchers' method is based on analysis of relative abundance curves, not sites ranked according to a known human-influence gradient, the behavior of their taxa richness metric cannot be attributed exclusively to human impact. Further, it is inappropriate to extrapolate from the presumed behavior of one metric to the behavior of all metrics in a multimetric index.

Subsamples of only 100 individuals are less likely than large samples to consistently reveal the presence of intolerant, long-lived, or otherwise rare taxa, regardless of their size; small subsamples are also likely to affect rela-tive abundances of key trophic or other ecological groups (Ohio EPA 1988).

Failing to count rare taxa or rare ecological groups such as intolerant taxa would exclude some of the strongest biological signals about the condition of places (Cao et al. 1998). This effect of subsampling is analogous to the exclusion of rare species that is often recommended in multivariate analyses (Reynoldson and Rosenberg 1996; see Premise 33).

An analysis of random subsamples of stream invertebrates collected in Puget Sound lowland streams (Doberstein et al., unpubl. manuscript) yielded very different conclusions from those of Barbour and Gerritsen (1996). Using a bootstrap resampling protocol like that described by Fore et al. (1994), Doberstein et al. generated several hundred subsamples for each of several streams for 100-, 200-, 300-, 500-, and 700-individual sub-samples and for the entire complement of individuals collected in three 0.1-square-meter samples. (The field sampling procedures were those described in Box 2.) After determining the variance in parameter estimates (metric values) for the resulting distributions of random samples, Dober-stein et al. then asked how many distinct classes of biological condition could be detected, by each metric and for the integrative B-IBIs.

Using the 10-metric B-IBI shown in Table 11, Doberstein et al. could reliably discern an average of 5.1 classes of biological condition per metric (range, 1.6 to 15.0) when they counted full samples from minimally dis-turbed streams (Figure 43). This result compares favorably with the 3 class-es distinguished by the 5, 3, and 1 scoring protocol. In contrast, metric

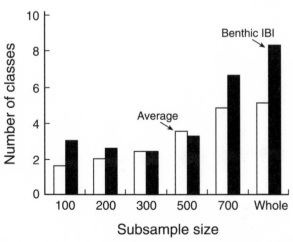

Figure 43. Average number of classes detected by metrics in a 10-metric B-IBI (see Table 11) and by the B-IBI itself at different subsample sizes. Data come from a minimally disturbed stream in King County, Washington.

sensitivity for random (bootstrap) 100-individual subsamples dropped to an average of 1.6 classes (range, 0.4 to 4.5). Counting all sampled individuals and then combining the metrics into a B-IBI permitted detection of 8.2 classes. Counting random 100-individual subsamples from each sample site, in contrast, allowed detection of only 2.8 classes of stream condition (see Figure 43). Doberstein et al. also found that counting an increasing number of 100-individual subsamples permitted detection of an increasing number of classes. For three minimally disturbed streams, counting three 100-individual subsamples instead of one raised the detectable levels of stream condition from 2.6 to 6.3 Would it not be simpler to count the whole sample to begin with?

In sum, one needs large enough samples and multiple metrics for a truly multimetric picture of biological condition. Multiple metrics together provide a stronger signal than one or two alone and, further, allow diagnosis of the likely causes of degradation.

Avoid thinking in regulatory dichotomies

The framework for environmental regulation necessarily divides actions and places into two: those that are "in compliance" and those that are not. Thinking in such either-or fashion pervades regulatory agencies: sites are viewed as "impaired" or "unimpaired," "acceptable" or "unacceptable," "safe" or "unsafe" (Murtaugh 1996). The legal standards and criteria for making these decisions are assumed to protect the overall condition of a site and its inhabitants.

The trouble is, biological condition is not an either-or affair. The condition of living systems within a region is a continuum, varying from near pristine to severely degraded. The biological condition of places thus falls along a gradient. Therefore, to fully understand, rank, and evaluate those places, researchers should also measure biological condition along a gradient (Ellis and Schneider 1997; see Premise 8). Biological condition is a continuous variable, so it should be measured on a continuous scale.

Multimetric biological indexes furnish a yardstick for measuring, tracking, evaluating, and communicating continuous variation in biological condition. Instead of simply labeling a site "control" or "treatment," "impaired" or "unimpaired," "acceptable" or "unacceptable," a multimetric assessment identifies and preserves finer biological distinctions among sites, in the index itself and in the values of the component metrics. Multimetric assessment automatically takes account of a site's context, permitting distinctions among urban streams that might all be labeled "impaired" in a dichotomous analysis. Suburban Swamp Creek sites near Seattle, for example, have B-IBIs of 26 to 34, which is clearly better than urban Thornton Creek's range of 10 to 18 but not nearly as good as rural Rock Creek's 44 to 46.

Dichotomous methods for evaluating biological condition lead to a variety of analytical and even regulatory problems. What is or is not an "acceptable" threshold in some biological (or chemical) factor depends on a site's context. Thresholds considered acceptable in an urban stream may be totally unacceptable in a rural or wildland stream. In addition, threshold definitions change over time as science and human values change, as people learn

more, and as measurement techniques become more sophisticated. Through
the years, the regulated community, as well as regulators and other citizens,
has become frustrated by what it perceives to be arbitrary moving targets in
the form of "minimum detectable" thresholds.

In contrast, measuring biological condition with a continuous yardstick
such as IBI puts a site along a continuum of condition in comparison with
other sites or other times, allowing thresholds to be reset according to context. It also permits a ranking of many sites—which might all be labeled
"degraded" in a dichotomous scheme—so that priorities may be set for
budget-constrained protection or restoration efforts.

Reference condition
must be defined properly

The goal of biological assessment is to detect and understand change in biological systems that results from the actions of human society. But change with respect to what? Just as economic analyses define a standard (e.g., 1950 dollars) against which economic activity can be judged, biological assessment must have a standard against which the conditions at one or more sites of interest can be evaluated. This standard, or reference condition, provides the baseline for site evaluation.

In multimetric biological assessment, reference condition equates with biological integrity—defined as the condition at sites able to support and maintain a balanced, integrated, and adaptive biological system having the full range of elements and processes expected for a region. Biological integrity is the product of ecological and evolutionary processes at a site in the relative absence of human influence (Karr 1996; Premise 6); IBI thus explicitly incorporates biogeographic variation. Protecting biological integrity is a primary objective of the Clean Water Act. The value of IBI is that it enables us to detect and measure divergence from biological integrity. When divergence is detected, society has a choice: to accept divergence from integrity at that place and time, or to restore the site.

Programs that measure biological and geophysical conditions in near-pristine environments provide much information about biotas and geophysical contexts in different areas. They inform managers about natural ranges of variation and allow comparisons across watersheds and landscapes among streams of similar elevation, size, or channel type; they provide ecologists with needed information about the interplay of physical processes and biological responses. But reference condition is only half the picture. If the goal of water resource management is to halt degradation of living aquatic systems, then managers must stop looking exclusively at natural processes and responses, as they have for many years in trying to implement biological criteria. Reference information is not enough.

Furthermore, measuring pristine conditions in one ecoregion or subecoregion after another, year after year, will not slow the degradation of aquatic resources. Sampling pristine environments from every ecoregion or subecoregion does not necessarily add insight about which biological attributes provide reliable signals about resource condition. Putting as much effort into quantifying and evaluating human influence as into collecting biogeographical information is the only way to discern biological signal from the background of natural variation. Sampling sites across a range of human influence provides the means to detect that signal.

The message here is clear. Agency biologists would do well to devote as much effort to understanding how to detect human influence as to collecting biogeographical "reference" information. Until state and federal agencies understand the importance of sampling across a gradient, both time and money will be wasted.

One major challenge is that there are few, if any, places left that have not been influenced by human actions. Thus, defining and selecting reference sites, and measuring conditions at those sites, require a careful sampling and analysis plan. Definition of reference condition may use modern or historical data, or theoretical models (Hughes 1995). Common pitfalls include using local sites that are degraded rather than looking over a wider area for minimally disturbed sites; arbitrarily defining reference sites without adequate screening or site evaluation; and ranking sites inaccurately so that degraded sites are put into reference sets. The problems are especially severe if arbitrary statistical rules are used to guide regulatory or other management decisions (e.g., Barbour et al. 1996a). If, for example, any site is considered "impaired" if its measured condition equals 25% of reference condition ("quartile range decision rules"), 25% of the reference sites would be considered impaired, even if they are not (Hannaford and Resh 1995).

The Wyoming Department of Environmental Quality misclassified its reference sites but was able to remedy the problem. The department had requested nominations for reference streams from water resource personnel in the state. Later, an analysis of biological data from 14 nominated sites (Patterson 1996) indicated that three sites had IBI values substantially below true reference condition, and sources of the sites' degradation were easily identified. Six additional sites also had low scores, suggesting some human-induced degradation. The remaining five Wyoming reference sites were not likely affected to any significant degree by human activity. Because properly defining reference condition is vital to the success of multimetric indexes, reference sites *must* be minimally influenced by people.

To make biological monitoring more effective—that is, to get information in the most cost-effective manner that can begin to protect water resources immediately—biologists need to document and understand dose-response relationships between particular biological attributes and human influence (see Premise 8). They need to identify metrics that respond to human disturbance and not just to geographical differences among ecoregions. They must shift their emphasis from exhaustively characterizing ecoregions or defining reference condition to sampling sites that have been subject to different intensities and types of human influence. Finally, they must choose a small set of metrics that provide reliable signals about the effects of human activities in the region. Metrics must be chosen according to their ability to distinguish between different types and intensities of human actions. By integrating those metrics into a multimetric index, we have a scientifically sound and policy-relevant tool to improve the management of water resources.

Statistical decision rules are no substitute for biological judgment

The objective of biological monitoring is to detect human-caused deviations from baseline biological integrity (see Premise 6 and Figure 4) and to evaluate the biological—not statistical—significance of those deviations and their consequences (Stewart-Oaten et al. 1986, 1992; Stewart-Oaten 1996). In other words, biological change, not p-value, is the endpoint of concern. A statistically significant result (small p-value) may not equate with a large, important effect, as researchers often assume; similarly, a statistically insignificant effect (large p-value) may well be biologically important (Yoccoz 1991; Stewart-Oaten 1996). Without some statement about the probability of detecting an effect of given magnitude, it is almost impossible for anyone to know for certain from, say, a t-test whether a biological effect is present. It is too simplistic, and potentially misleading, to assume that lack of statistical significance necessarily means that differences between places do not exist. Only power analysis can define the precision of a finding that two things do not differ.

Ecologists tend to overuse tests of significance (Yoccoz 1991). It is not enough to detect differences in lieu of determining an impact's magnitude and cause or in lieu of understanding its consequences (Stewart-Oaten 1996). It would be wiser to decide first what is biologically relevant and then use hypothesis testing to look for biologically relevant effects, not merely run a general "search for significance." Overreliance on statistical correlation, t-tests, or other statistical models can short-circuit the process of looking at data and asking whether they make sense and what they show. Dependence on p-values can divert scientists and managers from exploring the biology responsible for the patterns in data, no matter when or by whom they were collected.

To evaluate alternative decisions, scientists and managers should balance hypothesis testing with other statistical tools, such as decision theory (Hilborn 1997); they should explore thoroughly the causes and consequences of differences in biological condition. When a study is based on tested biological metrics, of course hypothesis testing can be appropriate, as when sites upstream and downstream of a point source need to be compared for setting regulations. But when a biologist or statistician reports a significant difference based on a p-value, the key next questions are, How different? In what way? What is the effect in biological systems?

By providing a biological yardstick for ranking sites according to their condition, multimetric indexes can answer these questions. Because their statistical properties are known and their statistical power can be calculated (see Premise 16; Peterman 1990; Fore et al. 1994), multimetric indexes can also be used to compare sites statistically. But a ranking according to biological condition is more appropriate than statistical comparisons for setting site-specific restoration or conservation priorities. Statistical significance is simply not the same as biological importance.

Multivariate statistical analyses often overlook biological knowledge

To many field biologists, "statistics" means "multivariate statistics" because field data are complex and multidimensional. Despite the availability of numerous statistical tools, monitoring studies have used the same multivariate techniques since the 1960s (Potvin and Travis 1993). These approaches—including cluster analysis, factor analysis, and widely used ordination techniques such as principal components analysis (PCA; James and McCulloch 1990)—extract the maximum statistical variance in variance-covariance matrices, usually across species or sites (Ludwig and Reynolds 1988). Unfortunately, the contexts in which multivariate methods have been applied have often precluded detecting, understanding, and basing decisions on some of the most important signals from biological systems.

The fault lies not with multivariate statistics themselves, which can provide important insights about the structure of data sets, but rather with how they are used. Multivariate analyses were developed for finding patterns, not assessing impacts. Failure to understand the difference, or to keep it in mind when interpreting biological data, can cause mistakes. We believe that misinterpretation is more common with multivariate techniques than with the multimetric approach. Certainly it is easier for people without statistical training to understand the results of a multimetric analysis. Many authors have covered the use of multivariate methods (Wright et al. 1993; Davies et al. 1995; Davies and Tsomides 1997; Walsh 1997), so this premise discusses some of the problems associated with their misuse in biological monitoring.

First, some ordination techniques, including PCA, assume that the data follow a multivariate normal distribution (Tabachnick and Fidell 1989), a pattern that is in fact rare in data from biological monitoring. These methods assume smooth continuous relationships, either a linear or simple polynomial pattern, but relationships among environmental variables are often nonlinear. In multivariate analysis, the numerous zeros and frequent high abundances typical of biomonitoring data show up as outliers with a potentially strong influence on the statistical solution (Gauch 1982; Tabachnick and Fidell 1989), so the data are often transformed to "fix" departures from normality, usually without success (Ter Braak 1986). Second, data are often edited (e.g., rare taxa are deleted), which may result in omitting important biological information (Walsh 1997; Cao et al. 1998).

Third, depending on which variables an analysis includes, multivariate techniques may fail to discriminate among important sources of variability, such as natural and human-induced variation or variation caused by sampling, subsampling, and error. Most multivariate data matrices contain a mix of sites, some with little influence from humans, others subject to different degrees of human influence. The matrices often mix data from different seasons or from, for example, different stream sizes or lake types. Although variables may be similarly confounded in multimetric analyses, it is usually easier to recognize and avoid this pitfall because multimetric analyses do not rely on computers to "discover" the relevant pattern.

Finally, multivariate approaches assume that statistically describing maximum variance will identify the most meaningful signal about biological condition. But because multivariate methods reduce the dimensionality of the original data by extracting or "loading" the maximum amount of variance on successive axes, they lose biological information at each step. This problem is compounded if the initial choice of biological variables was made without considering whether the variables responded across a continuum of human influence.

The most common applications of multivariate statistics rely on lists of taxa and their abundances to detect differences among sampled sites or times (Reynoldson and Metcalfe-Smith 1992; Norris and Georges 1993; Reynoldson and Zarull 1993; Norris 1995; Pan et al. 1996). PCA, for instance, uses mathematical algorithms to extract variance from a matrix of species abundances, one of the most variable aspects of biology, rather than examining how the animals feed, reproduce, use their habitat, or respond to human activities. When species-abundance matrices are the focus, important ecological attributes never even make it into the analysis. The combined loss of signal—because major important components of biology are ignored and because the statistical procedure cannot apportion variance to definable causes—limits the ability of the most common multivariate applications to discern complex patterns and to help investigators understand them.

In one telling example of the pitfalls of multivariate analyses of species abundances, two investigators advocated excluding rare species, saying that such species simply add "noise to the community structure signal and . . .

little information to the data analysis. . . . We recommend excluding all taxa that contribute less than 1% of the total number or occur at less that 10% of the sites" (Reynoldson and Rosenberg 1996: 5; see also Marchant 1989; Norris 1995).[9] Yet the presence of rare taxa indicates ecological conditions capable of supporting those often sensitive taxa; far from adding noise, rare taxa offer special clues about a site's environmental quality (Karr 1991; Courtemanch 1996; Fore et al. 1996; Cao et al. 1998).

Furthermore, comparing the results of PCA on real data with PCA on matrices of random numbers showed that the percentage of variance described may be similar for both, especially for the second and subsequent principal components; that loadings of original variables on principal axes are often as high for random numbers as for real data; and that matrix size is an important determinant of the amount of variance extracted (Karr and Martin 1981). Multivariate techniques were unable to discern known deterministic relationships in one study (Armstrong 1967), and in another, they manufactured relationships in data sets containing no such relationships (Rexstad et al. 1988).

PCA reflects the underlying linear correlation (or covariance) among all the variables in the matrix. If no, or small, correlations exist, then PCA can manufacture relationships. The problem can be avoided with a careful examination of the correlation matrix before applying PCA. Without careful choice of variables conveying reliable signals about biological condition or, as Gotelli and Graves (1996) argue, without a comparison of the data against a null model showing pattern(s) that would occur in the absence of any effect, multivariate statistics can misguide resource assessment efforts. General uses of PCA seldom give results that go beyond common sense (Karr and Martin 1981; Fore et al. 1996; Stewart-Oaten 1996). Gotelli and Graves (1996: 137) go so far as to suggest that "multivariate analysis has been greatly abused by ecologists. . . . [D]rawing polygons (or amoebas) around groups of species [or points], and interpreting the results often amounts to ecological palmistry. Ad hoc 'explanations' often are based on the original untransformed variables, so that the multivariate transformation offers no more insight than the original variables did."

The key danger of overreliance on multivariate analyses is that management decisions may be based on statistical properties of data—on the structure of a covariance matrix—rather than on biological knowledge and

[9] From the Ninth Annual Technical Information Workshop on study design and data analysis in benthic macroinvertebrate assessments (North American Benthological Society meeting, June 1996).

understanding. In fact, when multivariate analyses examine the same biological attributes used in multimetric indexes, they yield essentially identical results (Hughes et al. 1998). The key message, then, is to choose attributes and use procedures to account for biological impacts, not just to describe pattern. Avoid analytical "shortcuts" that are not easily understood or that must be done idiosyncratically for every data set. There is simply no substitute, either in multivariate statistics or in multimetric indexes, for careful application of biological and ecological knowledge. Careful design of sampling, thoughtful analysis of data, and careful description of biological condition can eliminate the need for general approaches that merely extract variance.

Assessing habitat cannot replace assessing the biota

In its broadest sense, *habitat* means the place where an organism lives, including all its physical, chemical, and biological dimensions; an oak-hickory forest or a cold-water stream is a habitat. Habitat also refers more narrowly to the physical structure of an environment. In streams, *habitat structure* generally means the physical structure of the channel and near-channel environment. Stream biologists see habitat structure as a critical component of environmental condition; they view habitat assessment, which involves measuring physical habitat structure, as a way to compare present structure with some idealized habitat.

Increasingly, scientists and managers have come to equate the presence of such idealized habitat with the presence of an organism; measuring habitat can even take the place of looking for the living inhabitants. But the presence of a given habitat structure does not guarantee the presence of desired biological inhabitants—any more than chemically clean water guarantees a biologically healthy stream. We are arrogant to assume that if we build "habitat," the inhabitants will come.

Stream habitat features include channel width and stability, water depth, streambed particle size, current velocity, and flow volume (Gorman and Karr 1978; Rankin 1995). These factors interact to define the mix of pools and riffles, pattern of meanders, or braiding characteristic of a stream channel. Width of the riparian area and floodplain, riparian canopy cover, bank condition, and woody debris are also important components of habitat structure.

Habitat assessments focus on such physical features to determine the suitability of a physical environment for an aquatic biota. In a habitat assessment, managers may measure the physical habitat directly, as in the habitat evaluation procedures developed by the U.S. Fish and Wildlife Service (FWS), or they may infer habitat condition from mathematical models, such as FWS's in-stream flow incremental method. Unfortunately, some have used these models to justify spending millions of dollars on "in-stream structure" without assessing biological responses or even the persistence of those structures in dynamic channels.

But habitat structure, like water quality, is only one of the five factors affected by human activities in a watershed (see Table 9). Severe physical damage to a stream channel is easy to see and document, but subtle degradation invisible to human observers may be biologically just as destructive. When resource agencies measure habitat variables in lieu of testing the response of living systems to human disturbance, they effectively assume that disturbance affects only physical habitat and that only visible damage harms a biota.

Yet measuring habitat structure may not reflect past sediment torrents or debris flows from upstream or from a road built along the channel. Habitat assessments do not reliably account for how floods or droughts are worsened by changes in the extent of impervious area in a watershed or the effects of water withdrawals. Connections with the hyporheic zone, where water flows within the streambed, are difficult to measure and poorly understood, yet the hyporheic zone is a critical refuge for some organisms during floods or drought. When groundwater flow patterns are altered by water withdrawal, these connections are broken; the consequences can be judged only by measuring the condition of the biota. Although simple biotic measures may not detect specific changes in the hyporheic zone, a biological change can lead to further investigations to identify the cause.

Measuring physical habitat cannot determine the effects on resident organisms of introduced and alien species, chemical contaminants, or changes in temperature or in dissolved oxygen. Measuring habitat structure in a stream where an invisible or unmeasurable form of water pollution is impairing the biota, for example, could lead one to conclude that the biota is healthy when it is not. Measures of stream habitat convey an incomplete picture of a stream's biological condition. Sampling water quality or habitat structure can aid in interpreting data on biological condition; it cannot and should not be used to define biological condition.

Fishery managers once neglected the physical structure of stream environments or considered it unimportant. But simply reversing that view is equally misguided. Habitat assessment alone does not capture all the ways that humans influence water resources. Using habitat surrogates to draw inferences about biological condition does not account for interactions between predators and prey, timing of peak or low flows, competition, alien species, or harvesting. Using habitat surrogates would be the analogy of a doctor's examining your home or workplace to see if you are sick, instead of examining you.

Worse, to talk of protecting "fish habitat" (or, more extreme, "fishery habitat") implies that we know what fish need; it implies that we can "fix" biological condition by fixing the habitat—by adding woody debris, building spawning channels, or bulldozing to create pools. Yet anadromous fish populations continue to decline in the Pacific Northwest despite expensive projects to restore stream channels and construct "spawning channels." A stream is more than a collection of habitat types. Physical habitat criteria are necessary, but entirely insufficient, to ensure even commodity production of wild salmon, let alone biological integrity.

Section V

Many Criticisms of Multimetric Indexes Are Myths

THE MULTIMETRIC APPROACH has come under fire from toxicologists, ecologists, and water managers on several grounds (Calow 1992; Suter 1993; Wicklum and Davies 1995). Yet numerous successful applications of multimetric biological monitoring and assessment (Yoder 1991a; Davis and Simon 1995; Lyons et al. 1995, 1996; Davis et al. 1996), explicit responses to the critics (Yoder 1991a; Karr 1993; Simon and Lyons 1995; Voshell et al. 1997; Hughes et al. 1998), and the work that led to this book suggest that biological criteria and multimetric indexes constitute robust tools for monitoring rivers and streams, especially when compared with the virtual lack of biological monitoring in the past.

"Biology is too variable to monitor"

The success of biological monitoring rests on our ability to select good indicators, ones sensitive to the underlying effects we want to measure—human influence—but insensitive to extraneous factors (Patil 1991). The belief that biology is too variable to monitor stems not from a lack of good indicators but from past failures to find the right indicators.

Because studies of naturally variable attributes such as population size, density, and abundance have dominated ecology for the better part of a century, resource managers as well as ecologists tend to regard biological assessments as less consistent than chemical assessments. But not all biological attributes vary as much as population size, density, and abundance; indeed, attributes such as traits of individuals or taxa richness yield clear, consistent patterns in response to human actions (see Premises 5 and 14). The issue, then, is not "biology vs. consistency" but, rather, which attributes of biology make sense to monitor: which attributes respond predictably to gradients of human influence? Measuring biological attributes that respond consistently gives important insights about the condition of water bodies.

The sources of variability in data—whether chemical, physical, or biological—must be controlled in field sampling protocols and laboratory procedures. Standardized lab procedures helped reduce the variability of chemical data but did not eliminate it. In the past decade, major advances have been made to standardize field biological sampling—in particular, to identify those biological attributes whose signal-to-noise ratio is high and that respond predictably to human impact.

Patterns in biological variation also offer some unexpected insights into human impact. Several studies have observed a correlation between mean and variance in IBI (see Premise 14): as IBI decreases, its variance increases (Karr et al. 1987; Steedman 1988; Rankin and Yoder 1990; Yoder 1991b). This association could reflect real changes in the resident biota at degraded sites, it could be a statistical artifact, or it may not be a general phenomenon. Hugueny et al. (1996), for example, reported lower variance in IBI from a disturbed site than from an upstream site. In the Willamette River, Oregon, standard deviations of IBI were highest at intermediate values (Hughes et al. 1998). Using the bootstrap algorithm, Fore et al. (1994) demonstrated that the increased variance of IBI values at degraded sites did reflect biological changes in the resident assemblage; this conclusion supports the observation that when biological systems are subjected to human disturbance, they are more variable. A thoughtful exploration of the specific circumstances in each of these cases might clarify these relationships.

Of course, natural variation cannot be separated entirely from human-induced variation, for human disturbance often exacerbates the effects of natural events (Schlosser 1990); floods or low flows are often more extreme in damaged watersheds, for example (Poff et al. 1997). The higher variance of IBI values observed at degraded sites (Karr et al. 1987; Steedman 1988; Fore et al. 1994; Yoder and Rankin 1995b) does point to effects on the sites' biological systems that mirror physical signs of degradation and suggests that highly variable IBIs may be an early-warning sign of excessive human impact.

"Biological assessment is circular"

Some have complained that IBI development is circular because biologists look at a site, decide whether it is degraded or pristine, and then develop metrics and an index that show the sites to be degraded or pristine as first observed. This view is flawed on two levels. On a concrete level, comparison of site condition with a regionally defined reference condition and assemblage—not one's own first observations—is built into metric testing and index development.

On a second, more abstract level, index development may appear circular because of the interplay between observation and experimentation that lies at the heart of science. Assessing water resources rarely allows replicated experiments; only one Puget Sound is available, for example, and controlled experiments at that scale are unlikely. Yet the links between certain human activities in watersheds and the biological health of the rivers running through those watersheds are clearly visible. As knowledge accumulates from repeated observation of real-world patterns, our confidence in the generality of those patterns increases.

Circularity can be avoided through repeated rigorous documentation of biological responses to a wide range of human actions (development of ecological dose-response curves) in a wide range of geographic areas. Ecological dose-response curves depict patterns that are both qualitative and quantitative, as well as consistent across a broad range of circumstances. For river fishes, for example, the same metrics (see Table 8) respond to human influence in studies in many habitats, under many human impacts, and for many regional assemblages (Miller et al. 1988; Lyons 1992a; Oberdorff and Hughes 1992; Hughes et al. 1998; Lyons et al. 1995, 1996). The same holds true for invertebrates (see Tables 6, 7, and 11). Indeed, many of the same attributes are consistent indicators for a variety of faunas (see Tables 5 and 11).

In her study of 115 streams in west-central Japan, Rossano (1995, 1996) convincingly demonstrated that IBI development is not circular; her work also verified dose-response patterns previously described for North America. Rossano first classified all 115 streams according to the type and magnitude of human activity within their watersheds (see Figure 5). After selecting a few streams that appeared the best and the worst, she randomly chose half the streams and plotted the quantitative values for biological attributes expected to change in those streams across her gradient of human influence (see Figure 6, top). She found distinct dose-response curves for some of the plotted metrics, including total taxa richness, number of intolerant taxa, number of clinger taxa, and relative abundance of tolerants (see Figure 15); these attributes also respond to human impact in North America. Rossano then scored these metrics (see Premise 15), summed the scores to yield a B-IBI for each site, and plotted the B-IBI values against human influence (see Figure 6, top). Finally, she applied the same metrics and scoring criteria from the first half of the data set to the other half of the 115 streams; B-IBIs from both sets of streams followed nearly identical patterns (see Figure 6, bottom; Rossano 1995, 1996).

Such systematic documentation and testing of metrics in many places and with many human influences reinforce the validity of those metrics and of the resulting IBIs as accurate yardsticks of human impact.

"We can't prove that humans degrade living systems without knowing the mechanism"

This comment implies that we must understand the means by which some-thing happens, not just *that* it happens, before we can act. We hear this com-ment from two rather different groups. The first is basic natural scientists, who focus on process and cause and effect and subscribe to the mantra of $\alpha = 0.05$ and the null hypothesis of no effect (Shrader-Frechette 1996). Rarely have these scientists been faced with day-to-day environmental deci-sion making. The second group embraces this view as a stalling tactic for overusing ecological systems, sidestepping their own responsibility while blaming "science" for knowing too little.

But where would medicine be now if doctors had to understand how diseases worked before treating them or how drugs worked before using them? For centuries, people have prevented or cured diseases and alleviated symptoms with drugs such as aspirin, even though they did not know the physiological mechanism by which the drugs acted. Modern med-icine recognizes and combats viral and bacterial diseases without fully understanding how each virus or bacterium does its damage. Humans rou-tinely act on the basis of what they see without knowing every mechanism behind it.

Of course, we want to know how observed changes come about in liv-ing systems altered by humans. But those mechanistic explanations are not essential for using biological monitoring to indicate degradation and find likely causes. The number of clinger taxa (or haptobenthos), for example, declines very reliably along gradients of human influence in Japan (Figure 44), in the Puget Sound lowlands (see Table 11), and in Virginia (Voshell et al. 1997), regardless of what we do or don't know about the specific mecha-nisms responsible. Perhaps fine sediments fill the spaces among cobbles, destroying the clingers' physical habitat. Perhaps clingers are more exposed

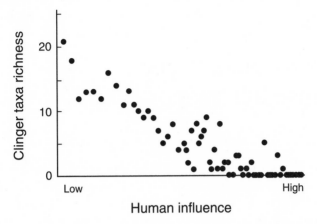

Figure 44. Number of clinger taxa plotted against a human influence gradient for Japanese streams (from Rossano 1995).

to predators as they move out of the sediment-laden spaces. Perhaps upwelling from hyporheic zones no longer supplies cool oxygenated water. Perhaps the diverse foods of many clinger species are no longer available. Perhaps all these factors are operating. Perhaps some other mechanism is responsible. But although the mechanism is not documented, the empirical pattern is clear: clinger taxa are disappearing. We would be foolish not to use this signal to detect degradation and to take protective actions.

"Indexes combine and thus lose information"

Because a multimetric index like IBI is a single numeric value, critics charge that the information associated with the metrics is somehow lost in calculating the index itself (U.S. EPA 1985; Suter 1993). Not at all.

Multimetric indexes condense, integrate, and summarize—they don't lose—information. They comprise the summed response signatures of individual metrics, which individually point to likely causes of degradation at different sites (Karr et al. 1986; Yoder 1991b; Yoder and Rankin 1995b). Although a single number, the index, is used to rank the condition of sites within a region, details about each site—expressed in the values of the component metrics—remain (Simon and Lyons 1995). It is straightforward to translate these numeric values into words describing the precise nature of each component in a multimetric evaluation. These descriptions, together with their numeric values, are available for making site-specific assessments, such as pinpointing sources of degradation (Yoder and Rankin 1995a) or identifying which attributes of a biotic assemblage are affected by human activities (see Figure 18).

At a site in urban Thornton Creek in Seattle, for example, total taxa richness is 25% of a reference stream minimally affected by human activity, Rock Creek in rural King County. Thornton Creek has only one mayfly taxon and no caddisflies or stoneflies, compared with five, six, and seven taxa of mayflies, caddisflies, and stoneflies, respectively, in Rock Creek. Individuals belonging to tolerant taxa make up more than 50% of the individuals in Thornton Creek samples and only 26% in Rock Creek samples. Thornton Creek has no long-lived or intolerant taxa, while Rock Creek supports four intolerant and two long-lived taxa. Rock Creek has a benthic IBI of 44 (maximum, 50), whereas Thornton Creek's IBI is only 10 (minimum, 10). Narrative descriptions of the sites as well as the numeric values for each metric and the B-IBI tell us a great deal about these two streams.

Those who advocate multivariate statistical analyses as the principal tool for biological monitoring insist that multimetric indexes lose information selectively. In their view, multivariate statistics extract biological patterns from the whole data set. Yet many multivariate analyses exclude rare taxa (see Premise 33), or they examine only species lists and abundances, an approach that overlooks organisms' natural history and ecology or the known responses of specific taxa to human actions. Multivariate statistical algorithms are based on the structure of variance-covariance matrices, not on specific knowledge of how organisms develop, find food, reproduce, and interact with one another and their physical and chemical surroundings.

Although management decisions can be, and have been, based on multivariate statistical analyses of biological data (Reynoldson and Zarull 1993; Wright et al. 1993; Davies et al. 1995), the decision process is hardly transparent to anyone who does not understand the mathematical algorithms or the models' underlying assumptions. In our view, multivariate statistics' inherent complexity distracts biologists from making clear, testable statements to one another and to nonscientists about how the biota of a place responds to human influence.

"Multimetric indexes aren't effective because their statistical properties are uncertain"

Although there may have been a basis for this statement at one time, later work on the statistical properties of biological data and of multimetric indexes suggests that, as for any other procedure, careful program design—from sampling and field work to data analysis—can yield data and conclusions that are both biologically useful and statistically robust. More important, perhaps, investigators have also shown that the problems associated with biological data of all kinds can be reduced by systematic planning, data collection, and analytical procedures. Conversely, when sampling design and data quality are not rigorously controlled, no procedure or approach can have known statistical properties.

In particular, bootstrap analysis of real data has demonstrated that the fish IBI approximates a normally distributed random variable (Fore et al. 1994; see Premise 16). In this study, the statistical precision of the fish IBI agrees with data collected over periods of two to eight years for both fish and invertebrates (Angermeier and Karr 1986; Karr et al. 1987). For example, 13 lowland Puget Sound streams were sampled at the same sites in successive years (1994–95) to evaluate between-year variation in the streams when human activities had not changed. B-IBI for these streams changed by no more than 4 during that two-year study; two sites increased by 2, four decreased by 2, three decreased by 4; and four were unchanged. All changed by 10% or less of the range of B-IBI, an exceptional stability for most biological analyses. Similar concordance among years was detected in studies in Oregon (R. M. Hughes, pers. commun.).

Statistical properties of multimetric indexes are known (see Premise 16), as are the sources of variability (see Premise 20). When one knows the sources of variability, one can construct studies to limit their influence. Too often biologists seek to incorporate all sources of variability rather than to design a study aimed at the kinds of variability relevant to program goals.

Biological monitoring has come a long way since the early 1980s in identifying the biological attributes to measure and in integrating these measures statistically in ways precise enough to describe the status and trends of biological systems. The declines in living aquatic systems tell us that we cannot afford to *not* use the tools we have or to stop seeking still better ones.

"A nontrivial effort is required to calibrate the index regionally"

This criticism hinges on the assumption that developing and using a multimetric biological index costs lots of time and money. True, the required effort is nontrivial, but how trivial is it to count permits issued, accumulate fines, collect samples, or produce "305(b) reports" that are not representative of regional or national conditions? How much money do agencies spend on these activities?

In fact, the cost of biological monitoring is often less than that of more conventional approaches (Yoder 1989; Table 12). Most important, the long-term cost of *not* doing effective biological monitoring is highest of all—the continued degradation and ultimate loss of the most valued components of life in our waters. "The specter of millions of dollars being misspent on environmental controls, without strong evidence of the efficacy of the treatment, indicates that money spent on high-quality monitoring programs is money well spent" (Rankin 1995).

During the last half of the 1990s, Karr and several graduate students developed and implemented region-specific biological standards in small streams and showed that biological responses to human actions can be documented and generally understood from studies lasting months, not years. Master of science students sampled about 30 sites in four months of field work, gathering enough data to define and calibrate a B-IBI after another three to six months of laboratory time and data analysis. Thus, geographic calibration can be accomplished within the time frame and budget of a master's project. Surely each region's water resources are worth that level of commitment.

Table 12. Comparative costs (in U.S. dollars) of collecting, processing, and analyzing samples to evaluate the quality of a water resource. (Data from Ohio EPA provided by C. O. Yoder.)

	Per sample[a]	Per evaluation[b]
Chemical and physical water quality		
4 samples per site	1436	8616
6 samples per site	2154	12,924
Bioassay		
Screening (acute 48-hour exposure)	1191	3573
Definitive (LC_{50}[c] and EC_{50},[d] 48- and 96-hour)	1848	5544
Seven-day (acute and chronic effects, 7-day exposure, single sample)	3052	9156
Seven-day (as above but with composite sample collected daily)	6106	18,318
Macroinvertebrate community	824	4120
Fish community	740	3700
Fish and macroinvertebrates combined	1564	7820

[a] Cost to sample one location or one effluent; standard evaluation protocols specify multiple samples per location.

[b] Cost to evaluate the impact of an entity; this example assumes sampling five stream sites and one effluent discharge.

[c] Dose of toxicant that is lethal to 50% of the organisms in the test conditions at a specified time.

[d] Concentration at which specified effect (e.g., hemorrhaging, pupil dilation, swimming cessation) is observed in 50% of tested organisms.

"The sensitivity of multimetric indexes is unknown"

This statement implies that multimetric indexes cannot discern and separate patterns of biological consequence from the noise of variation (natural, sampling, crew, seasonal, and so on). But the many examples described in this book show that a modest effort by a few people can systematically document biological patterns that are useful in research, management, and regulatory contexts. The key is to define ecological dose-response curves for a range of geographic areas and diverse human influences (logging, agriculture, recreation, and urbanization). We must connect human actions to biological change.

Section VI

The Future Is Now

Twenty-five years after passage of the Clean Water Act, we can be thankful that our rivers no longer catch fire. But the science of biological monitoring is still way ahead of the regulatory and policy framework used to manage water resources. The problem lies not in the letter or spirit of our laws but in a pervasive reluctance to shift from a narrow pollution-control mentality to a broader regard for the biological condition of our waters.

Humans tend to fiddle while Rome burns—not deliberately but because we react ineptly to complex situations. Faced with problems that exceed our grasp, we pile small error upon small error to arrive at spectacularly wrong conclusions (Dörner 1996). We did this when we built Egypt's Aswan Dam, disrupting a cycle of flooding and Nile Valley fertilization that had sustained farmers for millennia; we did it in the series of events leading up to the 1986 explosion of Reactor 4 at Chernobyl. Are we doomed to do it while our rivers, lakes, wetlands, and oceans get deeper into trouble?

We can and must translate biological condition into regulatory standards

When the 1972 amendments to the Water Pollution Control Act were being debated in Congress, then–EPA Administrator William Ruckelshaus testified in the House of Representatives against the House bill. Referring to its general objective to "restore and maintain . . . chemical, physical, and biological integrity," Ruckelshaus stated, "We do not support the new purpose or 'general objective' that would be provided. The pursuit of natural integrity for its own sake without regard to the various beneficial uses of water is unnecessary" (Committee on Public Works 1973). Later, after President Nixon had vetoed the amendments, the Senate Committee on Environment and Public Works underwent 33 days of hearings, 171 witnesses, 470 statements, 6400 pages of testimony, and 45 subcommittee and full-committee markup sessions—and concluded that "chronic adverse biological impact may be a greater problem than the acute results of discharge of raw sewage or large toxic spills" (Muskie 1992). The 1972 Water Pollution Control Act amendments finally passed, over the presidential veto, setting the restoration and maintenance of the biological integrity of water as the first of three broad goals.

For Ruckelshaus at the time, apparently, water "use" by humans was the whole story, and consumptive uses of water were legitimate while non-consumptive uses—such as keeping fish and wildlife alive, recreation, or aesthetics—were not sufficiently "beneficial." Like so many water resource managers before and since, the EPA administrator saw water as a fluid, a commodity to be bought and sold, not as a complex biological system that provides diverse benefits to society. For him and his agency, clean water was enough.

Clean water still seems to be enough for many in agency circles. Water resource managers schooled in the language and dogma of chemical pollution have been slow to adopt a broader view of resource degradation. Decision makers stay safely with existing rules and standards, most often interpreting them more narrowly than even the letter of the law suggests they should be interpreted. The federal and state agencies responsible for writing regulations, tracking water resource condition, and creating water-protecting incentives are reluctant to embrace biological integrity as a primary goal.

At present, water quality standards—the formalized rules regulators use to protect water resources—contain three components: designated uses, criteria, and the principle of antidegradation. (The antidegradation goal entered the regulatory agenda in the 1980s under the broad reasoning that water resource decisions should allow no further degradation. In theory, the antidegradation philosophy was supposed to end past acceptance of "dilution is the solution to pollution.") Under these rules, each state must define designated uses, or goals, for all water bodies within its boundaries. Criteria—generally numeric and chemical but sometimes narrative and biological (e.g., that conditions be "fishable and swimmable" or adequate to "protect aquatic life")—are then established. The assumption is that preventing violations of the criteria will protect the designated uses.

Chemical water quality measures, permits issued, and fines levied are still the primary currencies in most state water quality programs for protecting designated uses. The lion's share of water resource funding still goes to controlling point-source pollution, despite widespread knowledge that nonpoint pollution and nonchemical factors damage more miles of streams and acres of lakes than point sources do (see Table 9)—and this despite advances in biological monitoring that have laid a strong foundation for setting *numeric biological* criteria. It is past time to include biological monitoring, and the scientific assessment of resource condition it produces, into decision making. Biological criteria, and the regulations to implement them, would be better able to address society's present values and more appropriate for targeting expenditures to protect the quality of life in our waters and our communities.

As we have tried to show in this book, when supported by classification to minimize the heterogeneity of samples, an appropriate number of metrics proven to vary along a gradient of human influence, and standardized scoring procedures, multimetric biological monitoring and assessment can give decision makers clear signals about the condition of water resources—knowledge that is the essential first step toward wise targeting of expenditures to protect or restore those resources. So why have only two states incorporated biological monitoring and numeric biological criteria into water quality standards? Why have only 15 more begun to develop such criteria

(Davis et al. 1996)—despite calls to do so in the law, the scientific literature (Karr and Dudley 1981; Davis and Simon 1995), and the government's own documents (U.S. EPA 1988, 1990, 1996b)?

One may regard the glass as half full or half empty. Virtually no state had biological criteria in 1981 when the first multimetric fish IBI appeared (Karr 1981). And although adoption of numeric biological criteria has been slow (Davis et al. 1996), the 1990s brought some progress: by 1995, 29 states had narrative biological water quality standards, and 11 were developing them. Ohio, for example, was using the fish IBI and ICI, an invertebrate derivative of the fish IBI, to define two levels of biocriteria, excellent warm-water habitat and warm-water habitat, expressed as numeric standards. The criterion for excellent warm-water habitat was initially set at IBI = 50 for most of Ohio, to protect the state's highest-quality waters from additional degradation. Warm-water habitat (IBI > 40) applies to moderately degraded areas; this criterion is intended to prevent further degradation and provides an attainable benchmark for restoration of streams in watersheds that humans have heavily influenced.

Thus it is hardly farfetched to imagine use of biological criteria in all states. We have broad national objectives, reasonable criteria, and multimetric indexes that are biologically sound and statistically robust. Isn't it time for researchers and policymakers to stop arguing about whether we know enough to act definitively? Of course we don't know everything; of course water bodies, like forests, are more complicated than we *can* know. But we know a great deal. Perhaps we would make more progress in protecting our waters if researchers all agreed not to ask for further funding until regulatory agencies used the knowledge already piled up in their archives. Can we look forward to a lull in our research programs?

Citizens are changing their thinking faster than bureaucracies

Polls and a fast-rising number of grassroots watershed activities clearly show that the American people are aware of and concerned about the nation's rivers, lakes, wetlands, and oceans. Citizens are more informed scientifically than they were a couple of generations ago, and they are increasingly alarmed by what they see being lost from our waterways. People across the country identify water pollution as the most important environmental issue (e.g., in the Pacific Northwest; Harris and Associates 1995). U.S. coastal county and city managers have ranked safe, clean drinking water as number one among critical national issues (NOAA press release, May 1997, *www.noaa.gov/public-affairs*); indeed, 58% of these managers ranked clean water as equal to or more important than health care. In a survey conducted for American Rivers, 94% of respondents identified contamination of drinking water by sewage and industrial waste as a primary concern.

Such concerns have sparked thousands of citizen initiatives to monitor water quality and river health. The 1996–97 *River and Watershed Conservation Directory* (River Network 1996) lists some 3000 organizations and agencies in the United States whose missions directly address river or watershed protection. Mainstream organizations from the Izaak Walton League to Trout Unlimited have also expanded their view of rivers and river health. Local chapters of both these groups have begun to emphasize broader understanding of the causes and treatment of river degradation. New national organizations are developing as well. These include Great Rivers Environmental Education Network, Adopt-a-Stream Foundation, River Network, and River Watch Network (Karr et al., in press).

River monitoring done through the schools has become one of the fastest-growing elements of volunteer monitoring (U.S. EPA 1994c). Colorado Waterwatch, for example, is a partnership of the State Division of Wildlife and teachers and students at more than 250 schools; students monitor some 500 stations throughout Colorado. In Seattle, Washington, the Thornton Creek Alliance ties together the teachers and students in 28 elementary through high schools in a network, centered on rivers, with local business and political leaders. Rivers provide the theme for interdisciplinary education, and everyone gains a better understanding of local landscapes and a stronger sense of community.

At the same time, individual scientists and historically conservative scientific groups such as the American Fisheries Society, the Ecological Society of America, and the North American Benthological Society have expanded their efforts to reach governments and citizen groups. The Ecological Society, for example, has started a new series of publications, *Issues in Ecology,* targeted to the press, policymakers, and the public. The Benthological Society is establishing liaisons with major North American conservation organizations.

A curious, and telling, element in many citizen initiatives is that they are funded in part by local, state, and federal governments. King County, Washington, supports numerous citizen alliances seeking to learn more about their watersheds. A statewide Governor's Watershed Enhancement Board in Oregon makes substantial amounts of money available for local watershed initiatives. EPA has also funded numerous local groups to monitor and restore the condition of rivers. Why, we ask, are these agencies not doing more to broaden perspectives in their own ranks? Why are they not strengthening their own programs to track biological condition, as required under section 301(b) of the Clean Water Act?

If, as Dörner (1996) argues, failure has its own logic, that logic is seldom more obvious than in the workings of our bureaucracies. Humans long ago developed the tendency to deal with problems on an ad hoc basis. We defined and solved problems one at a time; we didn't need to see a situation embedded in the context of other situations; we thought in straight, cause-and-effect lines about one dimension at a time. Contemporary decision makers still (Dörner 1996: 18)

- Act without first analyzing the situation.

- Fail to anticipate side effects and long-term repercussions.

- Assume that the absence of immediately obvious negative effects means that correct measures have been taken.

- Let over-involvement in "projects" blind them to emerging needs and changes in the situation.

- Are prone to cynical reactions.

The inappropriateness of these reactions for solving modern problems is only made worse by the difficulty of separating good information from bad when we are overloaded with information; by our reluctance to accept new knowledge even when we see that it's good; and by defense of the status quo by bureaucracies and other vested economic, scientific, and political interests. This kind of approach worked fine in simpler, slower times; it doesn't work now in this complex, increasingly high-speed world. We need to respond quickly, and correctly, to our present environmental problems, but bureaucracies seem incapable of fast responses. If we really want to protect life in running waters, we must recognize the nature of modern organizational systems and hold them accountable (Bella 1997).

Some signs of hope are appearing, even from unlikely places such as government bureaucracies. Observing that "[t]he nation needs to know the status of its soil, water, air, plants, and animals and, if they are changing, why and how that change is taking place," a report from the National Science and Technology Council (1997) proposes a framework to integrate the nation's environmental monitoring and research programs. An intergovernmental task force on monitoring water quality has also developed a strategy for improving water quality monitoring in the United States. Both groups call for better biological monitoring. Sadly, these calls for action have yet to affect the day-to-day operations of environmental agencies.

In an editorial announcing the new electronic journal *Conservation Ecology*, Holling (1996) enumerated principles of a broader "integrative ecology" to link science, policy, and politics (see also Premise 6; Mayr 1997; Westra 1998). This integrative ecology is simple, broad, and exploratory. It relies on multiple lines of converging evidence. It considers multiple scales in time and space and how they interact. It weighs multiple competing hypotheses, considers the possibility that events have one or more causes that may or may not be separable, and is at home with uncertainty. It uses nonstandard statistics and worries as much about biological importance as about statistical significance (Mapstone 1996). Multimetric biological indexes do all of these things. They're an ideal tool for an integrative ecology.

Of course there are no magic solutions for overcoming our plodding ways of dealing with complex problems. But it helps to know how we think—that we sometimes think badly, that we often become stuck in old ways when new ways would be far better. It helps to realize that facing up to the next century's challenges does not necessarily require us to tap into some hitherto fallow 90% of our brain potential; rather, it requires the development of our common sense, our flexibility, our ability to anticipate consequences (Dörner 1996). Albert Einstein put it this way: "You cannot solve a problem by applying the same conceptual framework that created the problem." Environmental educator David Orr (1994) says simply, "Think at right angles." And use the best tools you can find.

Can we afford healthy waters? We can afford nothing less

Until all states see protecting biological condition as a central responsibility of water resource management, until they see biological monitoring as essential to track attainment of that goal and biological criteria as enforceable standards mandated by the Clean Water Act, life in the nation's waters will continue to decline.

We are all responsible, and we all need to do better. We must take a broader view of the problems we face if we hope to devise effective solutions. Citizens need to increase their understanding of science and continue to put pressure on governments to act. Scientists need to strengthen their biological monitoring approaches, talk with neighbors and relatives, write outside of technical publications, and dare to speak up in the realm of day-to-day decision making. Managers need to reexamine "the way it's always been done" and do what works to keep waters alive. Agency administrators need to allocate funding inside their own agencies to programs that actually protect water resources. They should redirect their agencies toward activities they are funding citizen watershed groups to do.

"Can we afford rivers and lakes and streams and oceans, which continue to make life possible on this planet?" If we answer yes to Edmund Muskie's question and act now to protect our last best waters and "restore and maintain the physical, chemical, and biological integrity" of the rest, the children of the twenty-first century might yet find life in running waters.

References

Adamus, P. R. 1996. *Bioindicators for Assessing Ecological Integrity of Prairie Wetlands.* EPA/600/R-96/082. U.S. Environmental Protection Agency, National Health and Environmental Effects Research Laboratory, Western Ecology Division, Corvallis, OR.

Allan, J. D., and A. S. Flecker. 1993. Biodiversity conservation in running waters. *Bioscience* 43: 32–43.

Allan, J. D., D. L. Erickson, and J. Fay. 1997. The influence of catchment land use on stream integrity across multiple spatial scales. *Freshwater Biol.* 37: 149–161.

Andersen, A. N. 1997. Using ants as bioindicators: Multiscale issues in a community ecology. *Conserv. Ecol.* 1: 8 (*www.consecol.org/vol1/iss1/art8*).

Anderson, M. P., and W. W. Woessner. 1992. *Applied Groundwater Modeling: Simulation of Flow and Advective Transport.* Academic Press, San Diego, CA.

Andreas, B. K., and R. W. Linchvar. 1995. Floristic index for establishing assessment standards: A case study for northern Ohio. *U.S. Army Waterways Exp. Stn. Tech. Rep.* WRP-DE-8.

Angermeier, P. L. 1997. Conceptual roles of biological integrity and diversity. Pages 49–65 in J. E. Williams, C. A. Wood, and M. P. Dombeck, eds. *Watershed Restoration: Principles and Practices.* American Fisheries Society, Bethesda, MD.

Angermeier, P. L., and J. R. Karr. 1986. Applying an index of biotic integrity based on stream fish communities: Considerations in sampling and interpretation. *N. Am. J. Fish. Manage.* 6: 418–429.

Angermeier, P. L., and J. R. Karr. 1994. Biological integrity versus biological diversity as policy directives. *Bioscience* 44: 690–697.

Angermeier, P. L., and I. J. Schlosser. 1995. Conserving aquatic biodiversity. *Am. Fish. Soc. Symp.* 17: 402–414.

Angermeier, P. L., and R. A. Smogor. 1995. Estimating number of species and relative abundances in stream-fish communities: Effects of sampling effort and discontinuous spatial distribution. *Can. J. Fish. Aquat. Sci.* 52: 936–949.

Armitage, P. D., D. Moss, J. F. Wright, and M. T. Furse. 1983. The performance of a new biological water quality score system based on macroinvertebrates over a wide range of unpolluted running-water sites. *Water Res.* 17: 333–347.

Armstrong, J. S. 1967. Derivation of theory by means of factor analysis, or Tom Swift and his electric factor analysis machine. *Am. Stat.* 21: 17–21.

Auerbach, A. J. 1982. The index of leading indicators: "Measurement without theory," thirty-five years later. *Rev. Econ. Stat.* 64: 589–595.

Augspurger, C. 1996. Editor's note. *Ecology* 77: 1698.

Bahls, L. L. 1993. *Periphyton Bioassessment Methods for Montana Streams.* Water Quality Bureau, Department of Health and Environmental Sciences, Helena, MT.

Ballentine, R. K., and L. J. Guarraia, eds. 1977. *The Integrity of Water: A Symposium.* U.S. Environmental Protection Agency, Washington, DC.

Barbour, M. T., and J. Gerritsen. 1996. Subsampling of benthic samples: A defense of the fixed-count method. *J. N. Am. Benthol. Soc.* 15: 386–391.

Barbour, M. T., J. L. Plafkin, B. P. Bradley, C. G. Graves, and R. W. Wisseman. 1992.

Evaluation of EPA's rapid bioassessment benthic metrics: Metric redundancy and variability among reference stream sites. *Environ. Toxicol. Chem.* 11: 437–449.

Barbour, M. T., J. B. Stribling, and J. R. Karr. 1995. Multimetric approach for establishing biocriteria and measuring biological condition. Pages 63–77 in W. S. Davis and T. P. Simon, eds. *Biological Assessment and Criteria: Tools for Water Resource Planning and Decision Making.* Lewis, Boca Raton, FL.

Barbour, M. T., J. Gerritsen, G. E. Griffith, R. Frydenborg, E. McCarron, and J. S. White. 1996a. A framework for biological criteria for Florida streams using benthic macroinvertebrates. *J. N. Am. Benthol. Soc.* 15: 185-211.

Barbour, M. T., J. B. Stribling, J. Gerritsen, and J. R. Karr. 1996b. *Biological Criteria: Technical Guidance for Streams and Small Rivers.* EPA 822-B-96-001. U.S. Environmental Protection Agency, Washington, DC.

Barbour, M. T., J. Gerritsen, B. D. Snyder, and J. B. Stribling. *Revision to Rapid Bioassessment Protocols for Use in Streams and Rivers: Periphyton, Benthic Macroinvertebrates, and Fish.* EPA 841-D-97-002. U.S. Environmental Protection Agency, Washington, DC (in press).

Beals, E. W. 1973. Ordination: Mathematical elegance and ecological naïveté. *J. Ecol.* 61: 23–35.

Bella, D. E. 1997. Organizational systems and the burden of proof. Pages 617–638 in D. J. Stouder, P. A. Bisson, and R. J. Naiman, eds. *Pacific Salmon and Their Ecosystems: Status and Future Options.* Chapman and Hall, New York.

Bisson, P. A., T. P. Quinn, G. H. Reeves, and S. V. Gregory. 1992. Best management practices, cumulative effects, and long-term trends in fish abundance in Pacific Northwest river systems. Pages 189–232 in R. J. Naiman, ed. *Watershed Management: Balancing Sustainability and Environmental Change.* Springer-Verlag, New York.

Blackburn, T. M., J. H. Lawton, and J. N Perry. 1992. A method for estimating the slope of upper bounds of plots of body size and abundance in natural animal assemblages. *Oikos* 65: 107–112.

Blair, R. B. 1996. Land use and avian species diversity along an urban gradient. *Ecol. Appl.* 6: 506–519.

Blair, R. B. 1998. Birds and butterflies along an urban gradient: Surrogate taxa for assessing biodiversity. *Ecol. Appl.* 8 (in press).

Blair, R. B., and A. E. Launer. 1997. Butterfly diversity and human land use: Species assemblages along an urban gradient. *Biol. Conserv.* 80: 113–125.

Botkin, D. B. 1990. *Discordant Harmonies.* Oxford University Press, New York.

Bottom, D. L. 1997. To till the water: A history of ideas in fisheries conservation. Pages 569–597 in D. J. Stouder, P. A. Bisson, and R. J. Naiman, eds. *Pacific Salmon and Their Ecosystems: Status and Future Options.* Chapman and Hall, New York.

Boyle, T. P., G. M. Smillie, J. C. Anderson, and D. P. Beeson. 1990. A sensitivity analysis of nine diversity and seven similarity indices. *J. Water Pollut. Control Fed.* 62: 749–762.

Bradford, D. F., S. E. Franson, A. C. Neale, D. T. Heggem, G. R. Miller, and G. E. Canterbury. 1998. Bird species assemblages as indicators of biological integrity in Great Basin rangeland. *Environ. Monit. Assess.* 49: 1–22.

Brinson, M. A. 1993. A hydrogeomorphic classification for wetlands. *U.S. Army Waterways Exp. Stn. Tech. Rep.* WRP-DE-4.

Brinson, M. A., and R. Reinhardt. 1996. The role of reference wetlands in functional assessment and mitigation. *Ecol. Appl.* 6: 69–76.

Brooks, R. P., and R. M. Hughes. 1988. Guidelines for assessing the biotic communities of freshwater wetlands. Pages 276–282 in J. A. Kusler, M. L. Quammen, and G. Brooks, eds. *Proceedings of the National Wetland Symposium: Mitigation of Impacts and Losses.* Association of State Wetland Managers, Berne, NY.

Calow, P. 1992. Can ecosystems be healthy? Critical consideration of concepts. *J. Aquat. Ecosyst. Health* 1: 1–5.

Cao, Y., A. W. Bark, and W. P. Williams. 1996. Measuring the responses of macroinvertebrate communities to water pollution: A comparison of multivariate approaches, biotic and diversity indices. *Hydrobiologia* 341: 1–19.

Cao, Y., W. P. Williams, and A. W. Bark. 1997. Similarity measure bias in river benthic Aufwuchs community analysis. *Water Environ. Res.* 69: 95–106.

Cao, Y., D. D. Williams, and N. E. Williams. 1998. How important are rare species in aquatic habitat bioassessment? *Bull. N. Am. Benthol. Soc.* 15: 109.

Carlisle, B. K., J. P. Smith, A. L. Hicks, B. G. Largay, and S. R. Garcia. 1998. *Wetland Ecological Integrity: An Assessment Approach.* Massachusetts Coastal Zone Management, Barnstable.

Carlson, C. A., and R. T. Muth. 1989. The Colorado River: Lifeline of the American Southwest. *Can. Spec. Publ. Fish. Aquat. Sci.* 106: 220–239.

Carpenter, S. R., D. Bolgrien, R. C. Lathrop, C. A. Stow, T. Reed, and M. A. Wilson. 1998. Ecological and economic analysis of lake eutrophication by nonpoint pollution. *Aust. J. Ecol.* 23: 68–79.

Casella, G., and R. L. Berger. 1990. *Statistical Inference.* Wadsworth, Belmont, CA.

Chu, E. W. 1997. Why assess ecological risk? *Environ. Health News,* winter: 3, 9. Department of Environmental Health, University of Washington, Seattle.

Chutter, F. M. 1972. An empirical biotic index of the quality of water in South African streams and rivers. *Water Resour.* 6: 19–30.

Colborn, T. E., and C. Clement, eds. 1992. *Chemically Induced Alterations in Sexual and Functional Development: The Wildlife-Human Connection.* Advances in Modern Environmental Toxicology 21. Princeton Scientific, Princeton, NJ.

Colborn, T. E., A. Davidson, S. N. Green, R. A. Hodge, C. I. Jackson, and R. A. Liroff. 1990. *Great Lakes, Great Legacy?* Conservation Foundation, Washington, DC.

Colborn, T. E., D. Dumanoski, and J. P. Myers. 1996. *Our Stolen Future: Are We Threatening Our Fertility, Intelligence, and Survival? A Scientific Detective Story.* Dutton, New York.

Committee on Public Works. 1973. *A Legislative History of the Water Pollution Control Act Amendments of 1972 Together with a Section-by-Section Index,* Vol. 1, serial no. 93-1. Environmental Policy Division, Congressional Research Service, Library of Congress. U.S. Government Printing Office, Washington, DC.

Costanza, R. 1992. Toward an operational definition of ecosystem health. Pages 239–256 in R. Costanza, B. G. Norton, and B. D. Haskell, eds. *Ecosystem Health: New Goals for Environmental Management.* Island Press, Washington, DC.

Costanza, R., and 12 others. 1997. The value of the world's ecosystem services and natural capital. *Nature* 387: 253–260.

Courtemanch, D. L. 1996. Commentary on the subsampling procedure used for rapid bioassessments. *J. N. Am. Benthol. Soc.* 15: 381–385.

CRESP (Consortium for Risk Evaluation with Stakeholder Participation). 1996. *CRESP at One Year: March 1995–1996.* Department of Environmental Health, University of Washington, Seattle.

Croonquist, M. J., and R. P. Brooks. 1991. Use of avian and mammalian guilds as indicators of cumulative impacts in riparian-wetland areas. *Environ. Manage.* 15: 701–704.

Cuffney, T. F., M. E. Gurtz, and M. R. Meador. 1993. Methods for collecting benthic invertebrate samples as part of the national water-quality assessment program. *U.S. Geol. Surv. Open File Rep.* 93-406.

Cummins, K. W. 1974. Structure and function of stream ecosystems. *Bioscience* 24: 631–641.

Cummins, K. W., M. A. Wilzbach, D. M. Gates, J. B. Perry, and W. B. Taliaferro. 1989. Shredders and riparian vegetation. *Bioscience* 39: 24–30.

Cummins, K. W., C. E. Cushing, and G. W. Minshall. 1995. Introduction: An overview of stream ecosystems. Pages 1–10 in C. E. Cushing, K. W. Cummins, and G. W. Minshall, eds. *River and Stream Ecosystems.* Elsevier, New York.

Cushman, R. M. 1984. Chironomid deformities as indicators of pollution from a synthetic coal-derived oil. *Freshwater Biol.* 14: 179–182.

Daily, G. C., ed. 1997. *Nature's Services: Societal Dependence on Natural Ecosystems.* Island Press, Washington, DC.

Danielson, T. J. 1998. *Indicators for Monitoring and Assessing Biological Integrity of Inland, Freshwater Wetlands: A Survey of Technical Literature* (1989–1996). EPA 843-R-98-002. Office of Wetlands, Oceans, and Watersheds, Office of Water, U.S. Environmental Protection Agency, Washington, DC.

Daubenmire, R. 1970. Steppe vegetation of Washington. *Wash. Agric. Exp. Stn. Tech. Bull.* 63.

Davies, S. P., and L. Tsomides. 1997. Methods for biological sampling and analysis of Maine's inland waters. DEP-LW107-A97. Maine Department of Environmental Protection, Augusta.

Davies, S. P., L. Tsomides, D. L. Courtemanch, and F. Drummond. 1995. Maine biological monitoring and biocriteria development program. Maine Department of Environmental Protection, Bureau of Land and Water Quality, Division of Environmental Assessment, Augusta.

Davis, W. S. 1995. Biological assessment and criteria: Building on the past. Pages 15–29 in W. S. Davis and T. P. Simon, eds. *Biological Assessment and Criteria: Tools for Water Resource Planning and Decision Making.* Lewis, Boca Raton, FL.

Davis, W. S., and T. P. Simon, eds. 1995. *Biological Assessment and Criteria: Tools for Water Resource Planning and Decision Making.* Lewis, Boca Raton, FL.

Davis, W. S., B. D. Snyder, J. B. Stribling, and C. Stoughton. 1996. Summary of state biological assessment programs for streams and rivers. EPA 230-R-96-007. Office of Policy, Planning, and Evaluation, U.S. Environmental Protection Agency, Washington, DC.

Deegan, L. A., J. T. Finn, S. G. Ayvasian, and C. Ryder. 1993. *Feasibility and Application of the Index of Biotic Integrity to Massachusetts Estuaries (EBI).* Massachusetts Executive Office of Environmental Affairs, Department of Environmental Protection, North Grafton.

Deegan, L. A., J. T. Finn, S. G. Ayvazian, C. A. Ryder-Kieffer, and J. Buonaccorsi. 1997. Development and validation of an estuarine biotic integrity index. *Estuaries* 20: 601–617.

DeShon, J. E. 1995. Development and application of the invertebrate community index (ICI). Pages 217–244 in W. S. Davis and T. P. Simon, eds. *Biological Assessment and*

Criteria: Tools for Water Resource Planning and Decision Making. Lewis, Boca Raton, FL.

Didier, J., and P. Kestemont. 1996. Relationships between mesohabitats, ichthyological communities, and IBI metrics adapted to a European river basin (The Meuse, Belgium). *Hydrobiologia* 341: 133–144.

Doberstein, C. P., J. R. Karr, and L. L. Conquest. The effect of subsampling on the effectiveness of macroinvertebrate biomonitoring (unpubl. manuscript).

Donahue, J. M., and B. R. Johnston, eds. 1998. *Water, Culture, and Power: Local Struggles in a Global Context.* Island Press, Washington, DC.

Dörner, D. 1996. *The Logic of Failure: Why Things Go Wrong and What We Can Do to Make Them Right.* Holt, New York.

Dufrêne, M., and P. Legendre. 1997. Species assemblages and indicator species: The need for a flexible asymmetrical approach. *Ecol. Monogr.* 67: 345–366.

Ebel, W. J., C. D. Becker, J. W. Mullan, and H. L. Raymond. 1989. The Columbia River: Toward a holistic understanding. *Can. Spec. Publ. Fish. Aquat. Sci.* 106: 205–219.

Ellis, J. I., and D. C. Schneider. 1997. Evaluation of a gradient sampling design for environmental impact assessment. *Environ. Monit. Assess.* 48: 157–172.

Engle, V. D., J. K. Summers, and G. R. Gaston. 1994. A benthic index of environmental condition of Gulf of Mexico estuaries. *Estuaries* 17: 372–384.

Erhardt, A., and J. A. Thomas. 1991. Lepidoptera as indicators of change in the seminatural grasslands of lowland and upland Europa. Pages 213–236 in N. M. Collins and J. A. Thomas, eds. *The Conservation of Insects and Their Habitats.* Academic Press, London.

Fausch, K. D., J. R. Karr, and P. R. Yant. 1984. Regional application of an index of biotic integrity based on stream fish communities. *Trans. Am. Fish. Soc.* 113: 39–55.

Fausch, K. D., J. Lyons, J. R. Karr, and P. L. Angermeier. 1990. Fish communities as indicators of environmental degradation. *Am. Fish. Soc. Symp.* 8: 123–144.

Fauth, J. E., J. Bernardo, M. Camara, W. J. Resetarits, Jr., J. Van Buskirk, and S. A. McCollom. 1996. Simplifying the jargon of community ecology: A conceptual approach. *Am. Nat.* 147: 282–286.

Ferraro, S. P., and F. A. Cole. 1990. Taxonomic level and sample size sufficient for assessing pollution impacts on the Southern California Bight macrobenthos. *Mar. Ecol. Prog. Ser.* 67: 251–262.

Ferraro, S. P., and F. A. Cole. 1995. Taxonomic level sufficient for assessing pollution impacts on the Southern California Bight macrobenthos (revisited). *Environ. Toxicol. Chem.* 14: 1031–1040.

Ferraro, S. P., and F. A. Cole. 1997. Effects of DDT sediment-contamination on macrofaunal community structure and composition in San Francisco Bay. *Mar. Biol.* 130: 323–334.

Ferraro, S. P., F. A. Cole, W. A. DeBen, and R. C. Swartz. 1989. Power-cost efficiency of eight macrobenthic sampling schemes in Puget Sound, Washington, USA. *Can. J. Fish. Aquat. Sci.* 46: 2157–2165.

Ferraro, S. P., R. C. Swartz, F. A. Cole, and D. W. Schults. 1991. Temporal changes in the benthos along a pollution gradient: Discriminating the effects of natural phenomena from sewage-industrial wastewater effects. *Estuarine Coastal Shelf Sci.* 33: 383–407.

Ferraro, S. P., R. C. Swartz, F. A. Cole, and W. A. DeBen. 1994. Optimum macrobenthic sampling protocol for detecting pollution impacts in the Southern California Bight. *Environ. Monit. Assess.* 29: 127–153.

Ferretti, M. 1997. Forest health assessment and monitoring: Issues for consideration. *Environ. Monit. Assess.* 48: 45–72.

Florida DEP (Department of Environmental Protection). 1996. *Standard Operating Procedures for Biological Assessment.* Florida Department of Environmental Protection, Tallahassee.

Ford, J. 1989. The effects of chemical stress on aquatic species composition and community structure. Pages 99–144 in S. A. Levin, M. A. Harwell, J. R. Kelly, and K. D. Kimball, eds. *Ecotoxicology: Problems and Approaches.* Springer-Verlag, New York.

Fore, L. S., J. R. Karr, and L. L. Conquest. 1994. Statistical properties of an index of biotic integrity used to evaluate water resources. *Can. J. Fish. Aquat. Sci.* 51: 1077–1087.

Fore, L. S., J. R. Karr, and R. W. Wisseman. 1996. Assessing invertebrate responses to human activities: Evaluating alternative approaches. *J. N. Am. Benthol. Soc.* 15: 212–231.

Fore, L. S., J. R. Karr, and C. K. Tait. Riparian condition and stream invertebrates: Biomonitoring to guide management of rangelands (unpubl. manuscript).

Frey, D. G. 1977. Biological integrity of water: An historical approach. Pages 127–140 in R. K. Ballentine and L. J. Guarraia, eds. *The Integrity of Water: A Symposium.* U.S. Environmental Protection Agency, Washington, DC.

Frissell, C. A. 1993. Topology of extinction and endangerment of native fishes in the Pacific Northwest and California (USA). *Conserv. Biol.* 7: 342–354.

Gammon, J. R. 1976. The fish populations of the middle 340 km of the Wabash River. *Purdue Univ. Wat. Resour. Ctr. Tech. Rep.* 86.

Gammon, J. R., A. Spacie, J. L. Hamelink, and R. L. Kaesker. 1981. Role of electrofishing in assessing environmental quality of the Wabash River. Pages 307–324 in J. M. Bates and C. I. Weber, eds. *Ecological Assessments of Effluent Impacts on Communities of Indigenous Aquatic Organisms.* STP 730. American Society of Testing and Materials, Philadelphia.

Gauch, H. G. 1982. *Multivariate Analysis in Community Ecology.* Cambridge University Press, Cambridge, UK.

Gerritsen, J. 1995. Additive biological indices for resource management. *J. N. Am. Benthol. Soc.* 14: 451–457.

Gerritsen, J., and J. White. 1997. *Development of a Biological Index for Florida Lakes.* Prepared for the Florida Department of Environmental Protection. Tetra Tech, Owings Mills, MD.

Goodall, D. W. 1954. Objective methods for the classification of vegetation. III. An essay in the use of factor analysis. *Aust. J. Bot.* 2: 304–324.

Gorman, O. T., and J. R. Karr. 1978. Habitat structure and stream fish communities. *Ecology* 59: 507–515.

Gotelli, N. J., and G. R. Graves. 1996. *Null Models in Ecology.* Smithsonian Institution Press, Washington, DC.

Green, R. H. 1979. *Sampling Design and Statistical Methods for Environmental Biologists.* Wiley, New York.

Greenfield, D. W., F. Abdel-Hameed, G. D. Deckert, and R. R. Flinn. 1973. Hybridization between *Chrosomus erythrogaster* and *Notropis cornutus* (Pisces: Cyprinidae). *Copeia* 1973: 54–60.

Gregory, R. 1987. Nonmonetary measures of nonmarket fishery resource benefits. *Trans. Am. Fish. Soc.* 116: 374–380.

Gregory, S. V., and P. A. Bisson. 1997. Degradation and loss of anadromous salmonid habitat in the Pacific Northwest. Pages 277–314 in D. J. Stouder, P. A. Bisson, and R. J. Naiman, eds. *Pacific Salmon and Their Ecosystems: Status and Future Options.* Chapman and Hall, New York.

Hager, M., and L. Reibstein. 1997. The cell from hell: *Pfiesteria* strikes again in the Chesapeake Bay. *Newsweek,* 25 August: 63.

Hamilton, A. L., and O. A. Saether. 1971. The occurrence of characteristic deformities in the chironomid larvae of several Canadian lakes. *Can. Entomol.* 103: 363–368.

Hannaford, M. J., and V. H. Resh. 1995. Variability in macroinvertebrate rapid-bioassessment surveys and habitat assessments in a northern California stream. *J. N. Am. Benthol. Soc.* 14: 430–439.

Hannah, L., D. Lohse, C. Hutchinson, J. L. Carr, and A. Lankerani. 1994. A preliminary inventory of human disturbance of world ecosystems. *Ambio* 23: 246–250.

Harig, A. L., and M. B. Bain. 1998. Defining and restoring biological integrity in wilderness lakes. *Ecol. Appl.* 8: 71–87.

Harris, L., and Associates. 1995. A survey on environmental issues in the Northwest. *Bellingham Herald,* 23 April: A-1.

Hartwell, S. I. 1997a. Demonstration of a toxicological risk ranking method to correlate measures of ambient toxicity and fish community diversity. *Environ. Toxicol. Chem.* 16: 361–371.

Hartwell, S. I., ed. 1997b. *Workshop Proceedings: Biological Habitat Quality Indicators for Essential Fish Habitat.* National Marine Fisheries Service, Charleston, SC.

Hartwell, S. I., C. E. Dawson, E. Q. Durell, R. W. Alden, P. C. Adolphson, D. A. Wright, G. M. Coelho, J. A. Magee, S. Ailstock, and M. Norman. 1997. Correlation of measures of ambient toxicity and fish community diversity in Chesapeake Bay, USA, tributaries: Urbanizing watersheds. *Environ. Toxicol. Chem.* 16: 2556–2567.

Hartwell, S. I., C. E. Dawson, E. Q. Durell, R. W. Alden, P. C. Adolphson, D. A. Wright, G. M. Coelho, and J. A. Magee. 1998. Integrated measures of ambient toxicity and fish community diversity. *Ecotoxicology* 7: 19–35.

Haskell, B. D., B. G. Norton, and R. Costanza. 1992. What is ecosystem health, and why should we worry about it? Pages 3–20 in R. Costanza, B. G. Norton, and B. D. Haskell, eds. *Ecosystem Health: New Goals for Environmental Management,* Island Press, Washington, DC.

Hawkes, C. L., D. L. Miller, and W. G. Layher. 1986. Fish ecoregions of Kansas: Stream fish assemblage patterns and associated environmental correlates. *Environ. Biol. Fish* 17: 267–279.

Herman, K. D., L. A. Masters, M. R. Penskar, A. A. Reznicek, G. S. Wilhelm, and W. S. Brodowicz. 1997. Floristic quality assessment: Development and application in the state of Michigan. *Nat. Areas J.* 17: 265–279.

Hesse, L. W., J. C. Schmulback, J. M. Carr, K. D. Keenlyne, D. G. Unkenholz, J. W. Robinson, and G. E. Mestl. 1989. Missouri River fishery resources in relation to past, present, and future status. *Can. Spec. Publ. Fish. Aquat. Sci.* 106: 352–371.

Hilborn, R. 1997. Statistical hypothesis testing and decision theory in fisheries science. *Fisheries* 22(10): 19–20.

Hilborn, R., and M. Mangel. 1997. *The Ecological Detective: Confronting Models with Data.* Princeton University Press, Princeton, NJ.

Hilsenhoff, W. L. 1982. Using a biotic index to evaluate water quality in streams. *Wis. Dep. Nat. Res. Tech. Bull.* 132.

Holl, K. D. 1995. Nectar resources and their influence on butterfly communities on reclaimed coal surface mines. *Restor. Ecol.* 3: 76–85.

Holl, K. D. 1996. The effect of coal surface mine reclamation on diurnal lepidopteran conservation. *J. Appl. Ecol.* 33: 225–236.

Holl K. D., and J. J. Cairns, Jr. 1994. Vegetational community development on reclaimed coal surface mines in Virginia. *Bull. Torrey Bot. Club* 121: 327–337.

Holling, C. S. 1996. Two cultures of ecology. *Conserv. Ecol.* (*www.consecol.org/Journal/editorial/editorial/html*).

Howarth, R. W. 1991. Comparative responses of aquatic ecosystems to toxic chemical stress. Pages 169–195 in J. Cole, G. Lovett, and S. Findlay, eds. *Comparative Analyses of Ecosystems: Patterns, Mechanisms, and Theories.* Springer-Verlag, New York.

Hubbs, C. L. 1961. Isolating mechanisms in the speciation of fishes. Pages 5–23 in W. F. Blair, ed. *Vertebrate Speciation.* University of Texas Press, Austin.

Hughes, R. M. 1985. Use of watershed characteristics to select control streams for estimating effects of metal mining wastes on extensively disturbed streams. *Environ. Manage.* 9: 253–262.

Hughes, R. M. 1995. Defining acceptable biological status by comparing with reference conditions. Pages 31–48 in W. S. Davis and T. P. Simon, eds. *Biological Assessment and Criteria: Tools for Water Resource Planning and Decision Making.* Lewis, Boca Raton, FL.

Hughes, R. M., and J. R. Gammon. 1987. Longitudinal changes in fish assemblages and water quality in the Willamette River, Oregon. *Trans. Am. Fish. Soc.* 116: 196–209.

Hughes, R. M., and R. F. Noss. 1992. Biological diversity and biological integrity: Current concerns for lakes and streams. *Fisheries* 17(3): 11–19.

Hughes, R. M., and T. Oberdorff. 1998. Applications of IBI concepts and metrics to waters outside the United States. In T. P. Simon, ed. *Assessing the Sustainability and Biological Integrity of Water Resources Using Fish Communities.* Lewis, Boca Raton, FL (in press).

Hughes, R. M., and 15 others. 1993. Development of lake condition indicators for EMAP: 1991 pilot. Pages 7–90 in D. P. Larsen and S. J. Christie, eds. *EMAP: Surface Waters 1991 Pilot Report.* EPA-620-R-93-003. Office of Research and Development, U.S. Environmental Protection Agency, Corvallis, OR.

Hughes, R. M., P. R. Kaufmann, A. T. Herlihy, T. P. Kincaid, L. Reynolds, and D. P. Larsen. 1998. A process for developing and evaluating indices of fish assemblage integrity. *Can. J. Fish. Aquat. Sci.* 55 (in press).

Hugueny, B., S. Camara, B. Samoura, and M. Magassouba. 1996. Applying an index of biotic integrity based on fish assemblages in a West African river. *Hydrobiologia* 331: 71–78.

Hurlbert, S. H. 1971. The nonconcept of species diversity. *Ecology* 52: 577–586.

Huston, M. A. 1994. *Biological Diversity: The Coexistence of Species on Changing Landscapes.* Cambridge University Press, New York.

Jacobson, J. L., and S. W. Jacobson. 1996. Intellectual impairment in children exposed to polychlorinated biphenyls in utero. *N. Engl. J. Med.* 335: 783–789.

Jacobson, J. L., S. W. Jacobson, and H. E. B. Humphrey. 1990. Effects of in utero exposure to polychlorinated biphenyls and related contaminants on cognitive functioning in young children. *J. Pediatrics* 116: 38–45.

James, F. C., and C. E. McCullough. 1990. Multivariate analysis in ecology and systematics: Panacea or Pandora's box? *Annu. Rev. Ecol. Syst.* 21: 129–166.

Jenkins, R. E., and N. M. Burkhead. 1994. *The Freshwater Fishes of Virginia.* American Fisheries Society, Bethesda, MD.

Jennings, M. J., L. S. Fore, and J. R. Karr. 1995. Biological monitoring of fish assemblages in Tennessee Valley reservoirs. *Regul. Rivers Res. Manage.* 11: 263–274.

Jennings, M. J., J. Lyons, E. E. Emmons, G. R. Hatzenbeler, M. Bozek, T. D. Simonson, T. D. Beard Jr., and D. Fago. 1998. Toward the development of an index of biotic integrity for inland lakes in Wisconsin. In T. P. Simon, ed. *Assessing the Sustainability and Biological Integrity of Water Resources Using Fish Communities.* Lewis, Boca Raton, FL (in press).

Kanehl, P. D., J. Lyons, and J. E. Nelson. 1997. Changes in the habitat and fish community of the Milwaukee River, Wisconsin, following removal of the Woolen Mills Dam. *N. Am. J. Fish. Manage.* 17: 387–400.

Karr, J. R. 1981. Assessment of biotic integrity using fish communities. *Fisheries* 6(6): 21–27.

Karr, J. R. 1987. Biological monitoring and environmental assessment: A conceptual framework. *Environ. Manage.* 11: 249–256.

Karr, J. R. 1991. Biological integrity: A long-neglected aspect of water resource management. *Ecol. Appl.* 1: 66–84.

Karr, J. R. 1993. Measuring biological integrity: Lessons from streams. Pages 83–104 in S. Woodley, J. Kay, and G. Francis, eds. *Ecological Integrity and the Management of Ecosystems.* St. Lucie Press, Delray Beach, FL.

Karr, J. R. 1994. Thinking about salmon landscapes. Pages 2–12 in M. Keefe, ed. *Salmon Ecosystem Restoration: Myth and Reality.* American Fisheries Society, Corvallis, OR.

Karr, J. R. 1995a. Risk assessment: We need more than an ecological veneer. *Hum. Ecol. Risk Assess.* 1: 436–442.

Karr, J. R. 1995b. Clean water is not enough. *Illahee* 11: 51–59.

Karr, J. R. 1996. Ecological integrity and ecological health are not the same. Pages 100–113 in P. Schulze, ed. *Engineering within Ecological Constraints.* National Academy Press, Washington, DC.

Karr, J. R. 1998a. Rivers as sentinels: Using the biology of rivers to guide landscape management. Pages 502–528 in R. J. Naiman and R. E. Bilby, eds. *River Ecology and Management: Lessons from the Pacific Coastal Ecoregion.* Springer, New York.

Karr, J. R. 1998b. Defining and measuring river health. *Freshwater Biol.* (in press).

Karr, J. R. 1998c. *Seeking Suitable Endpoints: Biological Monitoring and Biological Criteria for Wetland Assessment.* Report to U.S. Environmental Protection Agency, Seattle.

Karr, J. R., and E. W. Chu. 1997. Biological monitoring: Essential foundation for ecological risk assessment. *Hum. Ecol. Risk Assess.* 3: 993–1004.

Karr, J. R., and D. R. Dudley. 1981. Ecological perspective on water quality goals. *Environ. Manage.* 5: 55–68.

Karr, J. R., and F. C. James. 1975. Eco-morphological configurations and convergent evolution in species and communities. Pages 258–291 in M. L. Cody and J. M. Diamond, eds. *Ecology and Evolution of Communities.* Harvard University Press, Cambridge, MA.

Karr, J. R., and B. L. Kerans. 1992. Components of biological integrity: Their definition and use in development of an invertebrate IBI. Pages 1–16 in T. P. Simon and W. S.

Davis, eds. *Environmental Indicators: Measurement and Assessment Endpoints.* EPA 905/R-92/003. U.S. Environmental Protection Agency, Chicago.

Karr, J. R., and T. E. Martin. 1981. Random numbers and principal components: Further searches for the unicorn. Pages 20–24 in D. Capen, ed. The use of multivariate statistics in studies of wildlife habitat. *U.S. For. Serv. Gen. Tech. Rep.* RM-87.

Karr, J. R., and T. Thomas. 1996. Economics, ecology, and environmental quality. *Ecol. Appl.* 6: 31–32.

Karr, J. R., R. C. Heidinger, and E. H. Helmer. 1985a. Sensitivity of the index of biotic integrity to changes in chlorine and ammonia levels from wastewater treatment facilities. *J. Water Pollut. Control Fed.* 57: 912–915.

Karr, J. R., L. A. Toth, and D. R. Dudley. 1985b. Fish communities of midwestern rivers: A history of degradation. *Bioscience* 35: 90–95.

Karr, J. R., K. D. Fausch, P. L. Angermeier, P. R. Yant, and I. J. Schlosser. 1986. Assessment of biological integrity in running waters: A method and its rationale. *Illinois Nat. Hist. Surv. Spec. Publ.* 5.

Karr, J. R., P. R. Yant, and K. D. Fausch. 1987. Spatial and temporal variability of the index of biotic integrity in three midwestern streams. *Trans. Am. Fish. Soc.* 116: 1–11.

Karr, J. R., D. N. Kimberling, and M. A. Hawke. 1997. Measuring ecological health, assessing ecological risks: Using the index of biological integrity at Hanford (a preliminary report). Ecological Health Task Group, Consortium for Risk Evaluation with Stakeholder Particpation, University of Washington, Seattle.

Karr, J. R., J. D. Allan, and A. C. Benke. River conservation in the United States and Canada. In P. J. Boon, B. R. Davies, and G. E. Petts, eds. *Global Perspectives on River Conservation.* Wiley, London, UK (in press).

Keeler, A. G., and D. McLemore. 1996. The value of incorporating bioindicators in economic approaches to water pollution control. *Ecol. Econ.* 19: 237–245.

Kennedy, A. D. 1997. Biological complexity confounds the separation of point- and nonpoint sources of human impact on the natural world. *Environ. Monit. Assess.* 48: 173–192.

Kentucky DEP (Department of Environmental Protection). 1993. *Methods for Assessing Biological Integrity of Surface Waters.* Kentucky Department of Environmental Protection, Division of Water, Frankfort.

Kerans, B. L., and J. R. Karr. 1994. A benthic index of biotic integrity (B-IBI) for rivers of the Tennessee Valley. *Ecol. Appl.* 4: 768–785.

Kerans, B. L., J. R. Karr, and S. A. Ahlstedt. 1992. Aquatic invertebrate assemblages: Spatial and temporal differences among sampling protocols. *J. N. Am. Benthol. Soc.* 11: 377–390.

Kiffney, P. M., and W. H. Clements. 1994. Effects of heavy metals on a macroinvertebrate assemblage from a Rocky Mountain stream in experimental microcosms. *J. N. Am. Benthol. Soc.* 13: 511–523.

Kleindl, W. J. 1995. A benthic index of biotic integrity for Puget Sound lowland streams, Washington, USA. MS thesis, University of Washington, Seattle.

Klemm, D. J., P. A. Lewis, F. Fulk, and J. M. Lazorchak. 1990. *Macroinvertebrate Field and Laboratory Methods for Evaluating the Biological Integrity of Surface Waters.* EPA-600-4-90-030. Environmental Monitoring and Support Laboratory, U.S. Environmental Protection Agency, Cincinnati.

Klemm, D. J., P. A. Lewis, F. Fulk, and J. M. Lazorchak. 1993. *Fish Field and Laboratory Methods for Evaluating the Biological Integrity of Surface Waters.* EPA-600-R-92-111.

U.S. Environmental Protection Agency, Environmental Monitoring and Support Laboratory, Cincinnati.

Knopman, D. S., and R. A. Smith. 1993. Twenty years of the Clean Water Act. *Environment* 35(1): 16–20, 34–41.

Koizumi, N., and Y. Matsumiya. 1997. [Assessment of stream fish habitat based on index of biotic integrity.] *Bull. Jpn. Soc. Fish. Oceanogr.* 61: 144–156.

Kolkwitz, R., and M. Marsson. 1908. Okologie der pflanzlichen saprobien. *Ber. Dtsch. Bot. Ges.* 26a: 505–519. (Translated 1967. Ecology of plant saprobia. Pages 47–52 in L. E. Kemp, W. M. Ingram, and K. M. Mackenthum, eds. *Biology of Water Pollution.* Federal Water Pollution Control Administration, Washington, DC.

Kremen, C. 1992. Assessing the indicator properties of species assemblages for natural areas monitoring. *Ecol. Appl.* 2: 203–217.

Larsen, D. P. 1995. The role of ecological sample surveys in the implementation of biocriteria. Pages 287–300 in W. S. Davis and T. P. Simon, eds. *Biological Assessment and Criteria: Tools for Water Resource Planning and Decision Making.* Lewis Publishing, Boca Raton, FL.

Larsen, D. P. 1997. Sample survey design issues for bioassessment on inland aquatic ecosystems. *Hum. Ecol. Risk Assess.* 3: 979–991.

Larsen, D. P., J. M. Omernik, R. M. Hughes, C. M. Rohm, T. R. Whittier, A. J. Kinney, A. L. Gallant, and D. R. Dudley. 1986. The correspondence between spatial patterns in fish assemblages in Ohio streams and aquatic ecoregions. *Environ. Manage.* 10: 815–828.

Larsen, D. P., K. W. Thornton, N. S. Urquhart, and S. G. Paulsen. 1994. The role of sample surveys for monitoring the condition of the nation's lakes. *Environ. Monit. Assess.* 32: 101–134.

Lenat, D. R. 1988. Water quality assessment of streams using a qualitative collection method for benthic macro-invertebrates. *J. N. Am. Benthol. Soc.* 7: 222–233.

Lenat, D. R. 1993. A biotic index for the southeastern United States: Derivation and list of tolerance values, with criteria for assigning water quality ratings. *J. N. Am. Benthol. Soc.* 12: 279–290.

Lenat, D. R., and J. K. Crawford. 1994. Effects of land use on water quality and aquatic biota of three North Carolina Piedmont streams. *Hydrobiologia* 294: 185–199.

Lenat, D. R., and D. L. Penrose. 1996. History of the EPT taxa richness metric. *J. N. Am. Benthol. Soc.* 13: 305–307.

Logie, J. W., D. M. Bryant, D. L. Howell, and J. A. Vickery. 1996. Biological significance of UK critical load exceedance estimates for flowing waters: Assessments of dipper *Cinclus cinclus* populations in Scotland. *J. Appl. Ecol.* 33: 1065–1076.

Ludwig, J. A., and J. F. Reynolds. 1988. *Statistical Ecology.* Wiley, New York.

Lyons, J. 1992a. Using the index of biotic integrity (IBI) to measure environmental quality in warmwater streams of Wisconsin. *U.S. For. Serv. Gen. Tech. Rep.* NC-149.

Lyons, J. 1992b. The length of stream to sample with a towed electrofishing unit when fish species richness is estimated. *N. Am. J. Fish. Manage.* 12: 198–203.

Lyons, J., S. Navarro-Perez, P. A. Cochran, E. Santana C., and M. Guzman-Arroyo. 1995. Index of biotic integrity based on fish assemblages for the conservation of streams and rivers in west-central Mexico. *Conserv. Biol.* 9: 569–584.

Lyons, J., L. Wang, and T. D. Simonson. 1996. Development and validation of an index of biotic integrity for coldwater streams in Wisconsin. *N. Am. J. Fish Manage.* 16: 241–256.

MacDonald, L. H., A. Smart, and R. C. Wissmar. 1991. *Monitoring Guidelines to Evaluate Effects of Forestry Activities on Streams in the Pacific Northwest and Alaska.* EPA/910/9-91-001. U.S. Environmental Protection Agency, Seattle.

Magurran, A. E. 1988. *Ecological Diversity and Its Measurement.* Princeton University Press, Princeton, NJ.

Mapstone, B. D. 1996. Scalable decision rules for environmental impact studies: Effect size, type I, and type II errors. *Ecol. Appl.* 5: 401–410.

Marchant, R. 1989. A subsampler for samples of benthic invertebrates. *Bull. Aust. Soc. Limnol.* 12: 49–52.

Maret, T. R., C. T. Robinson, and G. W. Minshall. 1997. Fish assemblages and environmental correlates in least-disturbed streams in the upper Snake River basin. *Trans. Am. Fish. Soc.* 126: 200–216.

Master, L. 1990. The imperiled status of North American aquatic animals. *Biodiversity Network News* (Nature Conservancy) 3(3): 1–2, 7–8.

Maxted, J. R. 1997. Biology, probability, and the obvious. *Hum. Ecol. Risk Assess.* 3: 955–965.

Maxted, J. R., S. B. Weisberg, J. C. Chaillou, R. A. Eskin, and F. W. Kutz. 1997. Ecological condition of dead-end canals of the Delaware and Maryland coastal bays. *Estuaries* 20: 319–327.

Mayr, E. 1997. *This Is Biology: The Science of the Living World.* Harvard University Press, Cambridge, MA.

McAllister, D. E., A. L. Hamilton, and B. Harvey. 1997. Global freshwater biodiversity: Striving for the integrity of freshwater ecosystems. *Sea Wind* 11(3): 1–140.

McCarron, E., and R. Frydenborg. 1997. The Florida bioassessment program: An agent for change. *Hum. Ecol. Risk Assess.* 3: 967–977.

McDonough, T. A., and G. D. Hickman. 1998. Reservoir fishery assessment index development: A tool for assessing ecological health in Tennessee Valley Authority impoundments. In T. P. Simon, ed. *Assessing the Sustainability and Biological Integrity of Water Resources Using Fish Communities.* Lewis, Boca Raton, FL (in press).

McFarland, B. H., B. H. Hill, and W. T. Willingham. 1997. Abnormal *Fragilaria* spp. (Bacillariophyceae) in streams impacted by mine drainage. *J. Freshwater Ecol.* 12: 141–149.

McGeoch, M. A., and S. L. Chown. 1998. Scaling up the value of bioindicators. *Trends Ecol. Evol.* 13: 46–47.

Meador, M. R., R. F. Cuffney, and M. E. Gurtz. 1993. Methods for sampling fish communities as part of the national water-quality assessment program. *U.S. Geol. Surv. Open File Rep.* 93-104.

Mearns, A. J., and J. Q. Wood. 1982. Forecasting effects of sewage solids on marine benthic communities. Pages 495–512 in G. F. Mayer, ed. *Ecological Stress and the New York Bight: Science and Management.* Estuarine Research Federation, Columbia, SC.

Meeuwig, J. J., and R. H. Peters. 1996. Circumventing phosphorus in lake management: A comparison of chlorophyll *a* predictions from land use and phosphorus models. *Can. J. Fish. Aquat. Sci.* 53: 1795–1806.

Meffe, G. K. 1992. Techno-arrogance and halfway technologies: Salmon hatcheries on the Pacific coast of North America. *Conserv. Biol.* 6: 350–354.

Megahan, W. F., J. P. Potyondy, and K. A. Seyedbagheri. 1992. Best management practices and cumulative effects from sedimentation in the South Fork Salmon River:

An Idaho case study. Pages 401–441 in R. J. Naiman, ed. *Watershed Management: Balancing Sustainability and Environmental Change.* Springer-Verlag, New York.

Mensing, D. M., S. M. Galatowitsch, and J. R. Tester. Anthropogenic effects on the biodiversity of riparian wetlands of a northern temperate landscape. *J. Environ. Manage.* (in press).

Meyer, J. L. 1997. Stream health: Incorporating the human dimension to advance stream ecology. *J. N. Am. Benthol. Soc.* 16: 439–447.

Miller, D. L., and 13 others. 1988. Regional applications of an index of biotic integrity for use in water resource management. *Fisheries* 13(5): 12–20.

Miller, R. R., J. D. Williams, and J. E. Williams. 1989. Extinctions of North American fishes during the past century. *Fisheries* 14(6): 22–38.

Mills, E. L., S. R. Hall, and N. K. Pauliukonis. 1998. Exotic species in the Laurentian Great Lakes: From science to policy. *Great Lakes Res. Rev.* 3(2): 1–7.

Minns, C. K., V. W. Cairns, R. G. Randall, and J. E. Moore. 1994. An index of biotic integrity (IBI) for fish assemblages in the littoral zone of Great Lakes areas of concern. *Can. J. Fish. Aquatic Sci.* 51: 1804–1822.

Minshall, G. W., R. C. Peterson, K. W. Cummins, T. L. Bott, J. R. Sedell, C. E. Cushing, and R. L. Vannote. 1983. Interbiome comparison of stream ecosystem dynamics. *Ecol. Monogr.* 51: 1–25.

Mitchell, W. C., and A. F. Burns. 1938. *Statistical Indicators of Cyclical Revivals.* National Bureau of Economic Research, New York.

Mosteller, F., and J. M. Tukey. 1977. *Data Analysis and Regression.* Addison-Wesley, Reading, MA.

Moyle, P. B., and R. A. Leidy. 1992. Loss of aquatic ecosystems: Evidence from fish faunas. Pages 127–169 in P. L. Fielder and S. K. Jain, eds. *Conservation Biology: The Theory and Practice of Nature Conservation, Preservation, and Management.* Chapman and Hall, New York.

Moyle, P. B., and J. E. Williams. 1990. Biodiversity loss in the temperate zone: Decline of the native fish fauna of California. *Conserv. Biol.* 4: 275–284.

Murtaugh, P. A. 1996. The statistical evaluation of ecological indicators. *Ecol. Appl.* 6: 132–139.

Muskie, E. S. 1972. Senate consideration of the report of the Conference Committee, October 4, 1972. *Amendment of the Federal Water Pollution Control Act.* U.S. Government Printing Office, Washington, DC.

Muskie, E. S. 1992. Testimony of Edmund S. Muskie before the Committee on Environment and Public Works, on the Twentieth Anniversary of Passage of the Clean Water Act. September 22, 1992. Reprinted as S. Doc. 104-17. *Memorial Tribute Delivered in Congress, Edmund S. Muskie, 1914–1996.* U.S. Government Printing Office, Washington, DC.

National Science and Technology Council. 1997. *Integrating the Nation's Environmental Monitoring and Research Networks and Programs: A Proposed Framework.* Committee on Environment and Natural Resources, National Science and Technology Council, Washington, DC.

Nehlsen, W., J. E. Williams, and J. A. Lichatowich. 1991. Pacific salmon at the crossroads: Stocks at risk from California, Oregon, Idaho, and Washington. *Fisheries* 16(2): 4–21.

Nelson, S. M., and M. E. Epstein. 1998. Butterflies (Lepidoptera: Papilionoidea and Hesperioidea) of Roxborough State Park, Colorado, USA: Baseline inventory, community attributes, and monitoring plan. *Environ. Monit. Assess.* 22: 287–295.

Nelson, W. G. 1990. Prospects for development of an index of biotic integrity for evaluating habitat degradation in coastal streams. *Chem. Ecol.* 4: 197–210.

Nelson, W. G., B. J. Bergen, B. Brown, and D. Campbell. 1997. Conceptual framework and indicators to assess the ecological integrity of estuarine systems. *Bull. Ecol. Soc. Am.* 78(4): 291.

Norris, R. H. 1995. Biological monitoring: The dilemma of data analysis. *J. N. Am. Benthol. Soc.* 14: 440–450.

Norris, R. H., and A. Georges. 1993. Analysis and interpretation of benthic surveys. Pages 234–286 in D. M. Rosenberg and V. H. Resh, eds. *Freshwater Biomonitoring and Benthic Macroinvertebrates.* Chapman and Hall, New York.

NRC (National Research Council). 1983. *Risk Assessment in the Federal Government: Managing the Process.* National Academy Press, Washington, DC.

NRC (National Research Council). 1994. *Science and Judgment in Risk Assessment.* National Academy Press, Washington, DC.

NRC (National Research Council). 1996. *Understanding Risk.* National Academy Press, Washington, DC.

Oberdorff, T., and R. M. Hughes. 1992. Modification of an index of biotic integrity based on fish assemblages to characterize rivers of the Seine-Normandie basin, France. *Hydrobiologia* 228: 117–130.

Ohio EPA (Environmental Protection Agency). 1988. *Biological Criteria for the Protection of Aquatic Life,* volumes 1–3. Ecological Assessment Section, Division of Water Quality Monitoring and Assessment, Ohio Environmental Protection Agency, Columbus.

Olsen, A. R., J. Sedransk, D. Edwards, C. A. Gotway, W. Leggett, S. Rathbun, K. H. Reckhow, and L. J. Young. Statistical issues for monitoring ecological and natural resources in the United States. *Environ. Monit. Assess.* (in press).

Omernik, J. M. 1995. Ecoregions: A spatial framework for environmental management. Pages 49–62 in W. S. Davis and T. P. Simon, eds. *Biological Assessment and Criteria: Tools for Water Resource Planning and Decision Making.* Lewis, Boca Raton, FL.

Omernik, J. M., and R. G. Bailey. 1997. Distinguishing between watersheds and ecoregions. *J. Am. Water Resour. Assoc.* 33: 935–949.

Orr, D. W. 1994. *Earth in Mind: On Education, Environment, and the Human Prospect.* Island Press, Washington, DC.

Osenberg, C. W., R. J. Schmitt, S. J. Holbrook, K. E. Abu-Saba, and A. R. Flegal. 1994. Detection of environmental impacts: Natural variability, effect size, and power analysis. *Ecol. Appl.* 4: 16–30.

Pacific Rivers Council. 1995. *A Call for a Comprehensive Watershed and Wild Fish Conservation Program in Eastern Oregon and Washington,* 2d ed. Pacific Rivers Council, Eugene, OR.

Paller, M. H. 1995a. Relationships among number of fish species sampled, reach length surveyed, and sampling effort in South Carolina coastal plain streams. *N. Am. J. Fish. Manage.* 15: 110–120.

Paller, M. H. 1995b. Interreplicate variance and statistical power of electrofishing data from low-gradient streams in the southeastern United States. *N. Am. J. Fish. Manage.* 15: 542–550.

Pan, Y., R. J. Stevenson, B. H. Hill, A. T. Herlihy, and C. B. Collins. 1996. Using diatoms as indicators of ecological conditions in lotic systems: A regional assessment. *J. N. Am. Benthol. Soc.* 15: 481–494.

Patil, G. P. 1991. Encountered data, statistical ecology, environmental statistics, and weighted distribution methods. *Environmetrics* 2: 377–423.

Patrick, R. 1992. *Surface Water Quality: Have the Laws Been Successful?* Princeton University Press, Princeton, NJ.

Patterson, A. J. 1996. The effect of recreation on biotic integrity of small streams in Grand Teton National Park. MS thesis, University of Washington, Seattle.

Peterman, R. M. 1990. Statistical power analysis can improve fisheries research and management. *Can. J. Fish. Aquat. Sci.* 47: 2–15.

Pielou, E. C. 1975. *Ecological Diversity.* Wiley, New York.

Pimentel, D., C. Wilson, C. McCullum, R. Huang, P. Dwen, J. Flack, Q. Tran, T. Saltman, and B. Cliff. 1997. Economic and environmental benefits of biodiversity. *Bioscience* 47: 747–757.

Pimm, S. L. 1991. *The Balance of Nature: Ecological Issues in the Conservation of Species and Communities.* University of Chicago Press, Chicago.

Pinel-Alloul, B., G. Methot, L. Lapierre, and A. Willsie. 1996. Macroinvertebrate community as a biological indicator of ecological and toxicological factors in Lake Saint-Francois (Quebec). *Environ. Pollut.* 91: 65–87.

Plafkin, J. L., M. T. Barbour, K. D. Porter, S. K. Gross, and R. M. Hughes. 1989. *Rapid Bioassessment Protocols for Use in Streams and Rivers: Benthic Macroinvertebrates and Fish.* EPA/440/4-89-001. Assessment and Water Protection Division, U.S. Environmental Protection Agency, Washington, DC.

Poff, N. L., J. D. Allan, M. B. Bain, J. R. Karr, K. L. Prestegaard, B. D. Richter, R. E. Sparks, and J. C. Stromberg. 1997. The natural flow regime: A paradigm for river conservation and restoration. *Bioscience* 47: 769–784.

Policansky, D. 1993. Application of ecological knowledge to environmental problems: Ecological risk assessment. Pages 35–71 in C. Cothern, ed. *Comparative Environmental Risk Assessment.* Lewis, Boca Raton, FL.

Potvin, C., and J. Travis, eds. 1993. Statistical methods: An upgrade for biologists. *Ecology* 74: 1614–1676.

Pringle, H. 1998. North America's wars. *Science* 279: 2038–2040.

Raloff, J. 1998. Drugged waters. *Sci. News* 153: 187–189.

Rankin, E. T. 1995. Habitat indices in water resource quality assessments. Pages 181–208 in W. S. Davis and T. P. Simon, eds. *Biological Assessment and Criteria: Tools for Water Resource Planning and Decision Making.* Lewis, Boca Raton, FL.

Rankin, E. T., and C. O. Yoder. 1990. The nature of sampling variability in the index of biotic integrity in Ohio streams. Pages 9–18 in W. S. Davis, ed. *Proceedings of the 1990 Midwest Pollution Control Biologists Meeting.* EPA 905-9-90-005. Environmental Sciences Division, U.S. Environmental Protection Agency, Chicago.

Rapport, D. J. 1989. What constitutes ecosystem health? *Perspect. Biol. Med.* 33: 120–132.

Rapport, D. 1998. Defining ecosystem health. Pages 18–33 in *Ecosystem Health.* Blackwell Science, Malden, MA.

Rapport, D., R. Costanza, P. R. Epstein, C. Gaudet, and R. Levins. 1998. *Ecosystem Health.* Blackwell Science, Malden, MA.

Regier, H. A. 1993. The notion of natural and cultural integrity. Pages 3–18 in S. Woodley, J. Kay, and G. Francis, eds. *Ecological Integrity and the Management of Ecosystems.* St. Lucie Press, Delray Beach, FL.

Rexstad, E. A., D. D. Miller, C. H. Flather, E. M. Anderson, J. H. Hupp, and D. R. Anderson. 1988. Questionable multivariate statistical inference in wildlife habitat and community studies. *J. Wildl. Manage.* 52: 794–798.

Reynoldson, T. B., and J. L. Metcalfe-Smith. 1992. An overview of the assessment of aquatic ecosystem health using benthic invertebrates. *J. Aquat. Ecosyst. Health* 1: 295–308.

Reynoldson, T. B., and D. M. Rosenberg. 1996. Sampling strategies and practical considerations in building reference data bases for the prediction of invertebrate community structure. Pages 1–31 in R. C. Bailey, R. H. Norris, and B. Reynoldson, eds. *Study Design and Data Analysis in Benthic Macroinvertebrate Assessments of Freshwater Ecosystems Using a Reference Site Approach.* Technical Information Workshop, North American Benthological Society, Kalispell, MT.

Reynoldson, T. B., and M. A. Zarull. 1993. An approach to the development of biological sediment guidelines. Pages 177–200 in S. Woodley, J. Kay, and G. Francis, eds. *Ecological Integrity and the Management of Ecosystems.* St. Lucie Press, Delray Beach, FL.

Richards, C. L., L. B. Johnson, and G. E. Host. 1996. Landscape-scale influences on stream habitats and biota. *Can. J. Fish. Aquat. Sci.* 53(suppl. 1): 295–311.

Richards, C. L., R. J. Haro, L. B. Johnson, and G. E. Host. 1997. Catchment and reach-scale properties as indicators of macroinvertebrate species traits. *Freshwater Biol.* 37: 219–230.

Rickard, W. H., and R. H. Sauer. 1982. Self-revegetation of disturbed ground in the deserts of Nevada and Washington. *Northwest Sci.* 56: 41–47.

Risk Commission (Presidential/Congressional Commission on Risk Assessment and Risk Management). 1997. *Framework for Environmental Health Risk Management.* Presidential/Congressional Commission on Risk Assessment and Risk Management, Washington, DC.

River Network. 1996. *1996–1997 River and Water Conservation Directory.* To-the-Point Publications, Portland, OR.

Rivera, M., and C. Marrero. 1994. Determinación de la calidad de las aquas en las cuencas hidrográficas, mediante la utilization del índice de integridad biotica (IIB). *Biollania* 11: 127–148.

Rodriguez-Olarte, D., and D. C. Taphorn. 1994. Los peces como indicadores biológicos: Aplicación del índice de integridad biótica en ambientes acuáticos de los llanos occidentales de Venezuela. *Biollania* 11: 27–56.

Rogers, L. E., R. E. Fitzner, L. L. Cadwell, and B. E. Vaughan. 1988. Terrestrial animal habitats and population responses. Pages 182–250 in W. H. Rickard, L. E. Rogers, B. E. Vaughan, and S. F. Liebetrau, eds. *Balance and Change in a Semi-arid Terrestrial Ecosystem.* Elsevier, New York.

Rossano, E. M. 1995. Development of an index of biological integrity for Japanese streams (IBI-J). MS thesis, University of Washington, Seattle.

Rossano, E. M. 1996. *Diagnosis of Stream Environments with Index of Biological Integrity* (in Japanese and English). Museum of Streams and Lakes, Sankaido Publishers, Tokyo.

Roth, N. E., J. D. Allan, and D. E. Erickson. 1996. Landscape influences on stream biotic integrity assessed at multiple spatial scales. *Landscape Ecol.* 11: 141–156.

Rowe, C. L., O. M. Kinney, A. P. Fiori, and J. D. Congdon. 1996. Oral deformities in tadpoles (*Rana catesbiana*) associated with coal ash deposition: Effects on grazing ability and growth. *Freshwater Biol.* 36: 723–730.

Scharf, F. S., F. Juanes, and M. Sutherland. 1998. Inferring ecological relationships from the edges of scatter diagrams: Comparison of regression techniques. *Ecology* 79: 448–460.

Schelske, C. L. 1984. In situ and natural phytoplankton assemblage bioassays. Pages 15–47 in L. E. Shubert, ed. *Algae As Ecological Indicators.* Academic Press, London.

Schindler, D. W. 1987. Determining ecosystem responses to anthropogenic stress. *Can. J. Fish. Aquat. Sci.* 44(suppl. 1): 6–25.

Schindler, D. W. 1990. Experimental perturbations of whole lakes as tests of hypotheses concerning ecosystem structure and function. *Oikos* 57: 25–41.

Schlosser, I. J. 1990. Environmental variation, life history attributes, and community structure in stream fishes: Implications for environmental management and assessment. *Environ. Manage.* 14: 621–628.

Schmitt, R. J., and C. W. Osenberg, eds. 1996. *Detecting Ecological Impacts: Concepts and Applications in Coastal Habitats.* Academic Press, San Diego, CA.

Scott, M. C., and L. W. Hall, Jr. 1997. Fish assemblages as indicators of environmental degradation in Maryland coastal streams. *Trans. Am. Fish. Soc.* 126: 349–360.

Scrimgeour, G. J., and D. Wicklum. 1996. Aquatic ecosystem health and integrity: Problems and potential solutions. *J. N. Am. Benthol. Society* 15: 254–261.

Seattle Times. 1996. Surface water getting dirtier: Uphill battle cleaning rivers, streams, lakes, says state. 10 July: B3.

Shrader-Frechette, K. 1996. Methodological rules for four classes of scientific uncertainty. Pages 12–39 in J. Lemons, ed. *Scientific Uncertainty and Environmental Problem Solving.* Blackwell Science, Cambridge, MA.

Simberloff, D., D. C. Schmitz, and T. C. Brown, eds. 1997. *Strangers in Paradise: Impact and Management of Nonindigenous Species in Florida.* Island Press, Washington, DC.

Simon, T. P., ed. 1998. *Assessing the Sustainability and Biological Integrity of Water Resources Using Fish Communities.* Lewis, Boca Raton, FL (in press).

Simon, T. P., and J. Lyons. 1995. Application of the index of biotic integrity to evaluate water resource integrity in freshwater ecosystems. Pages 245–262 in W. S. Davis and T. P. Simon, eds. *Biological Assessment and Criteria: Tools for Water Resource Planning and Decision Making.* Lewis, Boca Raton, FL.

Smith, E. P. 1994. Biological monitoring: Statistical issues and models. *Handb. Stat.* 12: 243–261.

Smith, E. P., D. Orvos, and J. Cairns, Jr. 1993. Impact assessment using before-after control-impact (BACI) models: Concerns and comments. *Can. J. Fish. Aquat. Sci.* 50: 627–637.

Sokal, R. R., and F. J. Rohlf. 1981. *Biometry,* 2d ed. Freeman, New York.

Spackman, S. C., and J. W. Hughes. 1995. Assessment of minimum stream corridor width for biological conservation: Species richness and distribution along mid-order streams in Vermont, USA. *Biol. Conserv.* 71: 325–332.

Statzner, B., H. Capra, L. W. G. Higler, and A. L. Roux. 1997. Focusing environmental management budgets on non-linear system responses: Potential for significant improvements to freshwater ecosystems. *Freshwater Biol.* 37: 463–472.

Steedman, R. J. 1988. Modification and assessment of an index of biotic integrity to quantify stream quality in southern Ontario. *Can. J. Fish. Aquat. Sci.* 45: 492–501.

Stemberger, R. S., and J. M. Lazorchak. 1994. Zooplankton assemblage responses to disturbance gradients. *Can. J. Fish. Aquat. Sci.* 51: 2435–2447.

Stemberger, R. S., A. T. Herlihy, D. L. Kugler, and S. G. Paulsen. 1996. Climatic forcing on zooplankton richness in lakes of the northeastern United States. *Limnol. Oceanogr.* 41: 1093–1101.

Stevens, W. K. 1998. One in every eight plant species is imperiled, survey finds. *New York Times,* 9 April: A1.

Stewart-Oaten, A. 1996. Goals in environmental monitoring. Pages 17–28 in R. J. Schmitt and C. W. Osenberg, eds. *Detecting Ecological Impacts: Concepts and Applications in Coastal Habitats.* Academic Press, San Diego, CA.

Stewart-Oaten, A., W. W. Murdoch, and K. R. Parker. 1986. Environmental impact assessment: "Pseudoreplication" in time? *Ecology* 67: 929–940.

Stewart-Oaten, A., J. R. Bence, and C. W. Osenberg. 1992. Assessing effects of unreplicated perturbations: No simple solutions. *Ecology* 73: 1396–1404.

Stohlgren, T. J., G. W. Chong, M. A. Kalkhan, and L. D. Schell. 1997. Rapid assessment of plant biodiversity patterns: A methodology for landscapes. *Environ. Monit. Assess.* 48: 25–43.

Summers, J. K., and V. Engle. 1993. Evaluation of sampling strategies to characterize dissolved oxygen conditions in Gulf of Mexico estuaries. *Environ. Monit. Assess.* 24: 219–229.

Summers, K., L. Folmar, and M. RodonNaveira. 1997. Development and testing of bioindicators for monitoring the condition of estuarine ecosystems. *Environ. Monit. Assess.* 47: 275–301.

Suter, G. W. 1993. A critique of ecosystem health concepts and indexes. *Environ. Toxicol. Chem.* 12: 1533–1539.

Swift, B. L. 1984. Status of riparian ecosystems in the United States. *Water Resour. Bull.* 20: 233–238.

Swink, F., and G. Wilhelm. 1994. *Plants of the Chicago Region,* 4th ed. Indiana Academy of Science, Indianapolis.

Tabachnick, B. G., and L. S. Fidell. 1989. *Using Multivariate Statistics,* 2d ed. HarperCollins, New York.

Tait, C. K., J. L. Li, G. A. Lamberti, T. N. Pearsons, and H. W. Li. 1994. Relationships between riparian cover and the community structure of high desert streams. *J. N. Am. Benthol. Soc.* 13: 45–56.

Taylor, B. R. 1997. Rapid assessment procedures: Radical reinvention or just sloppy science? *Hum. Ecol. Risk Assess.* 3: 1005–1016.

Ter Braak, C. J. F. 1986. Canonical correspondence analysis: A new eigenvector technique for multivariate direct gradient analysis. *Ecology* 67: 1167–1179.

Thoma, R. F. 1990. *A Preliminary Assessment of Ohio's Lake Erie Estuarine Fish Communities.* Division of Water Quality Planning and Assessment, Ecological Assessment Section, Ohio Environmental Protection Agency, Columbus.

Thoma, R. F., and C. O. Yoder. 1997a. Ohio's Lake Erie and lacustuary monitoring program. Pages 34–45 in S. I. Hartwell, ed. *Workshop Proceedings: Biological Habitat Quality Indicators for Essential Fish Habitat.* National Marine Fisheries Service, Charleston, SC.

Thoma, R. F., and C. O. Yoder. 1997b. The Ohio Environmental Protection Agency's biological monitoring program: IBI measures and their possible application to estuarine environments. Pages 46–77 in S. I. Hartwell, ed. *Workshop Proceedings: Biological Habitat Quality Indicators for Essential Fish Habitat*. National Marine Fisheries Service, Charleston, SC.

Thompson, B. A., and G. R. Fitzhugh. 1986. *A Use Attainability Study: An Evaluation of Fish and Macroinvertebrate Assemblages of the Lower Calcasieu River, Louisiana*. LSU-CFI-29. Center for Wetland Resources, Coastal Fisheries Institute, Louisiana State University, Baton Rouge. (See Miller et al. 1988 for a synopsis of this study.)

Thompson, P. B. 1995. *The Spirit of the Soil: Agriculture and Environmental Ethics*. Routledge, London.

Thomson, J. D., G. Weiblen, B. A. Thomson, S. Alfaro, and P. Legendre. 1996. Untangling multiple factors in spatial distributions: Lilies, gophers, and rocks. *Ecology* 77: 1698–1715.

Thorne, R. St. J., and W. P. Williams. 1997. The response of benthic invertebrates to pollution in developing countries: A multimetric system of bioassessment. *Freshwater Biol.* 37: 671–686.

Tufte, E. R. 1983. *The Visual Display of Quantitative Information*. Graphics Press, Cheshire, CT.

Tufte, E. R. 1990. *Envisioning Information*. Graphics Press, Cheshire, CT.

Tufte, E. R. 1997. *Visual Explanations*. Graphics Press, Cheshire, CT.

Underwood, A. J. 1991. Beyond BACI: Experimental designs for detecting human environmental impacts on temporal variations in natural populations. *Aust. J. Mar. Freshwater Res.* 42: 569–587.

Underwood, A. J. 1994. On beyond BACI: Sampling designs that might reliably detect environmental disturbances. *Ecol. Appl.* 4: 3–15.

U.S. EPA. 1985. *Technical Support Document for Conducting Use Attainability Studies*. Office of Water Regulations and Standards, Office of Water, U.S. Environmental Protection Agency, Washington, DC.

U.S. EPA. 1988. *WQS Draft Framework for the Water Quality Standards Program*. Draft 11-8-88. Office of Water, U.S. Environmental Protection Agency, Washington, DC.

U.S. EPA. 1990. *Biological Criteria: National Program Guidance for Surface Waters*. EPA 440-5-90-004. Office of Water Regulations and Standards, U.S. Environmental Protection Agency, Washington, DC.

U.S. EPA. 1992a. *National Water Quality Inventory: 1990 Report to Congress*. EPA-503/9-92/006. U.S. Environmental Protection Agency, Washington, DC.

U.S. EPA. 1992b. *Framework for Ecological Risk Assessment*. EPA/630/R-92/001. Risk Assessment Forum, U.S. Environmental Protection Agency, Washington, DC.

U.S. EPA. 1994a. *Ecological Risk Assessment Issue Papers*. EPA/630/R-94/009. Risk Assessment Forum, Office of Research and Development, U.S. Environmental Protection Agency, Washington, DC.

U.S. EPA. 1994b. *Peer Review Workshop Report on Ecological Risk Assessment Issue Papers*. EPA/630/R-94/008. Risk Assessment Forum, Office of Research and Development, U.S. Environmental Protection Agency, Washington, DC.

U.S. EPA. 1994c. *National Directory of Volunteer Environmental Monitoring Programs*. EPA 841-B-94-001. Office of Water, U.S. Environmental Protection Agency, Washington, DC.

U.S. EPA. 1995. *National Water Quality Inventory: 1994 Report to the Congress*. U.S. Environmental Protection Agency, Washington, DC.

U.S. EPA. 1996a. National listing of fish and wildlife consumption advisories. EPA-823-F-96-006 (four-page fact sheet), EPA-823-C-96-001 (five PC diskettes). U.S. Environmental Protection Agency, Washington, DC.

U.S. EPA. 1996b. *Liquid Assets: A Summertime Perspective on the Importance of Clean Water to the Nation's Economy.* EPA 800-R-96-002. Office of Water, U.S. Environmental Protection Agency, Washington, DC.

U.S. EPA. 1996c. *Environmental Indicators of Water Quality in the United States.* EPA 841-R-96-002. U.S. Environmental Protection Agency, Washington, DC.

U.S. EPA. 1996d. Proposed guidelines for ecological risk assessment: Notice. FRL-5605-9. *Federal Register* 61: 47552–47631.

U.S. EPA. 1998. Wetland bioassessment fact sheets. EPA 843-F-98-001. Office of Wetlands, Oceans, and Watersheds, Office of Water, U.S. Environmental Protection Agency, Washington, DC.

van Belle, G., G. S. Omenn, E. M. Faustman, C. W. Powers, J. A. Moore, and B. D. Goldstein. 1996. Dealing with Hanford's legacy. *Wash. Publ. Health* 14: 16–21.

Vannote, R. L., G. W. Minshall, K. W. Cummins, J. R. Sedell, and C. E. Cushing. 1980. The river continuum concept. *Can. J. Fish. Aquat. Sci.* 37: 130–137.

van Swaay, C. A. M. 1990. An assessment of the changes in butterfly abundance in The Netherlands during the twentieth century. *Biol. Conserv.* 52: 287–302.

Vinson, M. R., and C. P. Hawkins. 1996. Effects of sampling area and subsampling procedure on comparisons of taxa richness among streams. *J. N. Am. Benthol. Soc.* 15: 392–399.

Voshell, Jr., J. R., E. P. Smith, S. K. Evans, and M. Hudy. 1997. Effective and scientifically sound bioassessment: Opinions and corroboration from academe. *Hum. Ecol. Risk Assess.* 3: 941–954

Wallace, J. B., J. W. Grumbaugh, and M. R. Whiles. 1996. Biotic indices and stream ecosystem processes: Results from an experimental study. *Ecol. Appl.* 6: 140–151.

Walsh, C. J. 1997. A multivariate method for determining optimal subsample size in the analysis of macroinvertebrate samples. *Mar. Freshwater Res.* 48: 241–248.

Wang, L., J. Lyons, P. Kanehl, and R. Gatti. 1997. Influences of watershed land use on habitat quality and biotic integrity in Wisconsin streams. *Fisheries* 22(6): 6–12.

Ward, R. C., and J. C. Loftis. 1989. Monitoring systems for water quality. *Crit. Rev. Environ. Control* 19: 101–118.

Warwick, W. F., and N. A. Tisdale. 1988. Morphological deformities in *Chironomus, Cryptochironomus,* and *Procladius* (Diptera: Chironomidae) from two differentially stressed sites in Tobin Lake, Saskatchewan. *Can. J. Fish. Aquat. Sci.* 45: 1123–1144.

Warwick, W. F., J. Fitchko, P. M. McKee, D. R. Hart, and A. J. Bunt. 1987. The incidence of deformities in *Chironomus* spp. from Port Hope Harbour, Lake Ontario. *J. Great Lakes Res.* 13: 88–92.

Washington, H. G. 1984. Diversity, biotic, and similarity indices: A review with special relevance to aquatic ecosystems. *Water Res.* 18: 653–694.

Water Quality 2000. 1991. *Challenges for the Future: Interim Report.* Water Pollution Control Federation, Alexandria, VA.

Weaver, M. J., and L. A. Deegan. 1996. Extension of the estuarine biotic integrity index across biogeographic regions (abstract). *Bull. Ecol. Soc. Am.* (suppl.) 77(3): 472.

Weaver, M. J., J. J. Magnuson, and M. D. Clayton. 1993. Analyses for differentiating littoral fish assemblages with catch data from multiple sampling gears. *Trans. Am. Fish. Soc.* 122: 1111–1119.

Weisberg, S. B., J. A. Ranasinghe, L. C. Schaffner, R. J. Diaz, D. M. Dauer, and J. B. Frithsen. 1997. An estuarine benthic index of biotic integrity (B-IBI) for Chesapeake Bay. *Estuaries* 20: 149–158.

Westra, L. 1998. *Living in Integrity: A Global Ethic to Restore a Fragmented Earth*. Rowman and Littlefield, Lanham, MD.

White, R. J., J. R. Karr, and W. Nehlsen. 1995. Better roles for fish stocking in aquatic resource management. *Am. Fish. Soc. Symp.* 15: 527–547.

Whittier, T. R. 1998. Development of IBI metrics for lakes in southern New England. In T. P. Simon, ed. *Assessing the Sustainability and Biological Integrity of Water Resources Using Fish Communities*. Lewis, Boca Raton, FL (in press).

Whittier, T. R., R. M. Hughes, and D. P. Larsen. 1988. The correspondence between ecoregions and spatial patterns in stream ecosystems in Oregon. *Can. J. Fish. Aquat. Sci.* 45: 1264–1278.

Whittier, T., D. B. Halliwell, and S. G. Paulsen. 1997a. Cyprinid distributions in northeast USA lakes: Evidence of regional-scale minnow biodiversity losses. *Can. J. Fish. Aquat. Sci.* 54: 1593–1607.

Whittier, T. R., P. Vaux, G. D. Merritt, and R. B. Yeardley, Jr. 1997b. Fish sampling. In J. R. Baker, D. V. Peck, and D. W. Sutton, eds. *Environmental Monitoring and Assessment Program, Surface Waters: Field Operations Manual for Lakes*. EPA/620/R-97/001. U.S. Environmental Protection Agency, Washington, DC.

Wicklum, D., and R. W. Davies. 1995. Ecosystem health and integrity? *Can. J. Bot.* 73: 997–1000.

Wilcove, D. S., and M. J. Bean, eds. 1994. *The Big Kill: Declining Biodiversity in America's Lakes and Rivers*. Environmental Defense Fund, Washington, DC.

Wildhaber, M. L., and C. J. Schmitt. 1998. Indices of benthic community tolerance in contaminated Great Lakes sediments: Relations with sediment contaminant concentrations, sediment toxicity, and the sediment quality triad. *Environ. Monit. Assess.* 49: 23–49.

Wilhelm, G., and L. A. Masters. 1995. *Floristic Quality Assessment in the Chicago Region and Application Computer Programs*. Morton Arboretum, Lisle, IL.

Wilhm, J. L., and T. C. Dorris. 1968. Biological parameters for water quality criteria. *Bioscience* 18: 477–481.

Williams, J. D., M. L. Warren, Jr., K. S. Cummings, J. L. Harris, and R. J. Neves. 1993. Conservation status of freshwater mussels of the United States and Canada. *Fisheries* 18(9): 6–22.

Williams, J. E., and R. R. Miller. 1990. Conservation status of the North American fish fauna in fresh water. *J. Fish Biol.* 37(suppl. A): 79–85.

Williams, J. E., and R. J. Neves. 1992. Biological diversity in aquatic management. *Trans. N. Am. Wildl. Nat. Resour. Conf.* 57: 343–432.

Williams, J. E., J. E. Johnson, D. A. Hendrickson, S. Contreras-Balderas, J. D. Williams, M. Navarro-Mendoza, D. E. McAllister, and J. E. Deacon. 1989. Fishes of North America endangered, threatened, or of special concern: 1989. *Fisheries* 14(6): 2–20.

Williams, J. E., C. A. Wood, and M. P. Dombeck, eds. 1997. *Watershed Restoration: Principles and Practices*. American Fisheries Society, Bethesda, MD.

Williamson, M. H. 1981. *Island Populations*. Oxford University Press, Oxford, UK.

Winterbourn, M. J., J. S. Rounick, and B. Cowie. 1981. Are New Zealand stream ecosystems really different? *N. Z. J. Mar. Freshwater Res.* 15: 321–328.

Wolda, H. 1981. Similarity indices, sample size, and diversity. *Oecologia* 50: 296–302.

Wood, J. Q. 1980. Classification of benthic invertebrates into infaunal trophic index feeding groups. *South. Calif. Coastal Water Res. Proj. Bienn. Rep.* 1979: 103–121.

Wright, J. F., M. T. Furse, and P. D. Armitage. 1993. RIVPACS: A technique for evaluating the biological quality of rivers in the UK. *Eur. Water Pollut. Control* 3: 15–25.

Yoccoz, N. G. 1991. Use, overuse, and misuse of significance tests in evolutionary biology and ecology. *Bull. Ecol. Soc. Am.* 71: 106–111.

Yoder, C. O. 1989. The development and use of biological criteria for Ohio surface waters. Pages 139–146 in G. H. Flock, ed. *Water Quality Standards for the 21st Century.* Office of Water, U.S. Environmental Protection Agency, Washington, DC.

Yoder, C. O. 1991a. Answering some questions about biological criteria based on experiences in Ohio. Pages 95–104 in *Water Quality Standards for the 21st Century.* U.S. Environmental Protection Agency, Washington, DC.

Yoder, C. O. 1991b. The integrated biosurvey as a tool for evaluation of aquatic life use attainment and impairment in Ohio surface waters. Pages 110–122 in *Biological Criteria: Research and Regulation.* EPA-440-5-91-005. Office of Water, U.S. Environmental Protection Agency, Washington, DC.

Yoder, C. O., and E. T. Rankin. 1995a. Biological criteria program development and implementation in Ohio. Pages 109–144 in W. S. Davis and T. P. Simon, eds. *Biological Assessment and Criteria: Tools for Water Resource Planning and Decision Making.* Lewis, Boca Raton, FL.

Yoder, C. O., and E. T. Rankin. 1995b. Biological response signatures and the area of degradation value: New tools for interpreting multimetric data. Pages 263–286 in W. S. Davis and T. P. Simon, eds. *Biological Assessment and Criteria: Tools for Water Resource Planning and Decision Making.* Lewis, Boca Raton, FL.

Zakaria-Ismail, M. 1994. Zoogeography and biodiversity of the freshwater fishes of Southeast Asia. *Hydrobiologia* 285: 41–48.

Index

About the Authors

James R. Karr is a professor of fisheries and zoology and an adjunct professor of civil engineering, environmental health, and public affairs at the University of Washington, Seattle. He holds as B.S. in fish and wildlife biology from Iowa State University and an M.S. and Ph.D. in zoology from the University of Illinois, Urbana–Champaign. He was on the faculties of Purdue University, University of Illinois, and Virginia Tech University; he was also deputy director and acting director at the Smithsonian Tropical Research Institute in Panama. He has taught and done research in tropical forest ecology, ornithology, stream ecology, watershed management, landscape ecology, conservation biology, ecological health, and science and environmental policy. He is a fellow in the American Association for the Advancement of Science and the American Ornithologists' Union. Karr was founding coeditor, with Ellen Chu, of *Illahee: Journal for the Northwest Environment;* he has served on the editorial boards of *BioScience, Conservation Biology, Ecological Applications, Ecological Monographs, Ecology, Ecosystem Health, Freshwater Biology,* and *Tropical Ecology.* He has also written more than 200 scholarly articles, reports, book reviews, and popular essays on ecology and environment. He developed the index of biotic integrity (IBI) to directly evaluate the effects of human actions on the health of living systems.

Ellen W. Chu is the editorial director at Northwest Environment Watch, a Seattle-based research and publishing center working for a sustainable society in the Pacific Northwest. She holds an A.B. and Ph.D. in biology from the University of California, Santa Cruz, where she did research on animal behavior and on the ecology of marine birds and taught zoology and natural history; she also holds an M.S. from the University of Paris. She taught scientific and technical writing and science journalism at the Massachusetts Institute of Technology and was editor-in-chief of the American Institute for Biological Sciences' journal *BioScience,* for which she won an Olive Branch award for outstanding coverage of the nuclear arms issue. She has edited numerous books and articles in the biological sciences, environmental studies, science and society, and computer technology; publishers include Academic Press, Microsoft Press, Northwest Environment Watch, and Wadsworth. Chu was founding coeditor, with James Karr, of *Illahee: Journal for the Northwest Environment* and the writer and editor of *Environmental Health News,* both published by the University of Washington. She is a member of the editorial boards of *Cascadia Times* and the Council of Biology Editors' *CBE Views.* She has written many reports, book reviews, editorials, and scientific and popular articles.